Powering UP

A History of the Women of the Union Pacific in North Platte, Nebraska

Published by Odd Duck Press
1005 North Dewey Street
North Platte, NE 69101

Printed in the United States of America

Book Design by Kai Crozer

Cover © 2011 by Ronald E. Lukesh

Front Cover Photo of Goldie and Martha Johansen by Marjorie Taylor

Back Cover Photo by Christy Callendar (daughter of Frances Gledhill)

Library of Congress Control Number: 2011912294
Milton, Ann E.

Powering UP / by Ann E. Milton

p. cm.

Summary: History of the women of the Union Pacific from 1908 to 2011 in North Platte, Nebraska

ISBN 978-0-9763676-7-3

Acknowledgements

The women who told their stories made this book possible. Their fearlessness and joy inspired me. My hat (though not a hard one) is off to each woman who shared her personal experience.

Many thanks also to:

The Original Town Association

The Union Pacific Railroad

Brenda Mainwaring, Director, Public Affairs, UPRR

Kaycee Anderson and the North Platte Public Library

Jim Griffith and the Lincoln County Historical Museum

Eric Seacrest and the Mid-Nebraska Community Foundation

Marjorie Taylor, photographer of the 1940s

John Bromley and the Union Pacific Railroad Museum, Council Bluffs, IA

The Lincoln County Clerk's Office

Lyle Minshull and the North Platte Parks Department

Sharon Owen and the A to Z Bookstore

North Platte Telegraph

North Platte Bulletin

Dave Harrold, Don Kurre, Ron Snell, Morgan Greenwood, Hope Hunt, Lori Clinch, Jeanette Pappas, Rose Mary Buhrman, Janice Martin, Camille Phelps, Mary Ann Carson, John Townsend and Kathy Marquette

And the relatives who shared memories and photos of those they loved.

Preface

The primary purpose of this book is to honor the achievements and contributions of women to the Union Pacific Railroad and to show how the Union Pacific improved their lives in return.

Time constraints limited the project to women who worked in the North Platte Yard. Privacy issues limited it to those women who contacted the researchers.

Hoffhine's Directory in the North Platte Public Library lists the residents of North Platte and their occupations beginning in 1907. The set of directories is not complete, but it was a valuable source of names of women who worked for Union Pacific in the early years— not that there were many. Unfortunately, if a woman was married, her husband's occupation was listed, but hers (if she had one) was not. Despite their incompleteness, the directories provide a revealing glimpse of occupations for women in North Platte at the turn of the 20th century. There were women teachers, maids, salesladies, telephone operators, students, housekeepers, bakers, cooks, seamstresses, nurses, dressmakers, milliners, clerks, hotel employees, cleaners, cashiers, bookkeepers, reporters, printers, boarding house keepers, servants, office assistants, stenographers and not much else.

Minnie McCoy was the only woman found employed by Union Pacific before WWI. She is listed as a stenographer in 1907. That is the only year her name appears.

There is a sudden influx of names in 1917 as WWI created a need for workers. There is just as sudden a decline after the war. By 1928 the number of female railroad employees in North Platte had dwindled to one: Florence Stamp. She persisted and became the first woman in North Platte to retire from Union Pacific.

In 1942 war again opened doors that were previously closed to women. The end of WWII brought a gradual decrease in the number of women working, but more managed to keep their jobs than after the first war.

The era of Affirmative Action in the 1970s opened the floodgates. Today women can be found in almost all occupations offered by Union Pacific. Perhaps one day a woman will be president of the company.

Ann E. Milton

Contents

Section I

The Women of World War I to 1941

Introduction

The United States entered World War I in April 1917. In July, General John J. Pershing put in a request for 3 million more men. Workers all over the country left their jobs to fight. Women were recruited to fill the open positions in every industry, including the railroad. They did not replace engineers, but thousands joined the workforce as clerks or telegraphers or engine cleaners.

According to historian Maurine Greenwald in her book *Women, War and Work*, by the time the war ended in November of 1918 more than 100,000 women were employed in railroad jobs.

It would seem that the surge in women's employment outside the home would be a victory for the women's rights movement and propel women to greater independence, but this was not the case. The campaign that began with the Women's Rights Convention in July 1848 in the small town of Seneca Falls, New York, lost focus after World War I. Having gained the right to vote in 1920 with the passage of the Nineteenth Amendment, many women felt they had achieved liberation. Even though a number of women did not exercise their right to vote and many voted as instructed by their husbands, the cause championed by Lucretia Mott, Elizabeth Cady Stanton, Susan B. Anthony, Sojourner Truth, Carrie Chapman Catt, Emma Goldman, Charlotte Perkins Gilman and Alice Paul fragmented and lost vision. Such a concentrated effort as the Women's Rights Movement would not be seen again until the 1960s.

The Union Pacific Railroad in North Platte acquired its share of women employees in clerical and communication positions, but less than ten years after the war's end, only Florence Stamp remained.

I do not believe that women are better than men. We have not wrecked railroads, nor corrupted legislature, nor done many unholy things that men have done; but then we must remember that we have not had the chance.
— Jane Addams

First Female Union Pacific Employee

Minnie McCoy

Minnie McCoy was a stenographer for Union Pacific in 1907. She was the first woman found listed as employed by the railroad in North Platte.

Telephone Operators

Lena Wangen Lowe

Lena Wangen was born in Aurland, Norway, in 1886. She came to the United States on a 14-day steamer trip with her aunt and uncle as chaperones. Lena lived with the family of Boomer Brown, an engineer on the railroad.

Lena learned telegraphy at Barnes Business School in Denver. She was employed as a telegrapher, stenographer and telephone operator for Union Pacific (UP) during WWI.

While working for the railroad, Lena met Theo Jr. (Pete) Lowe who had started with UP when he was 14. Lena and Pete had two children, Robert and Don.

When Lena quit in 1918, Florence Stamp took her place.

Lena died in 1972 and is buried in the North Platte Cemetery.

Florence Stamp

In 1917 Louise Florence Stamp was a telephone operator for Western Union. When Union Pacific began hiring women to replace men leaving to fight in the war in 1918, she hired on as a telephone operator and began a career that lasted nearly 40 years.

Florence was the first woman to retire from Union Pacific service in North Platte. At a ceremony commemorating her retirement in 1957, Vic Beloit, manager of the telegraph and PBX office, presented her with a television set. She also received a scroll with the names of those who had contributed to the purchase of the television.

Sharron Hewgley, the daughter of Edna Brown who worked with Florence, shared her memories of Florence, "She was extremely kind and well thought of. She never forgot my birthday, my Christmas or any occasion. She was big on giving books. I think I had every Bobbsey Twins book published and I got them as gifts from her."

For many years Florence was the only woman employed by Union Pacific in North Platte.

Florence never married. She died in 1964 and is buried in the North Platte Cemetery.

Alma Brodbeck

Alma Brodbeck was a telephone operator for Union Pacific in 1925.

Katie Deidel (1940s photo courtesy of Marjorie Taylor)

Crew Caller

Catherine C. Tatom Beloit Deidel Paul

Catherine C. Tatom was born in 1903. She was only 16 during WWI, but she is listed in the North Platte Directory as a messenger (crew caller) for Union Pacific. She was hired again during WWII as a fireman/oiler and worked in the old roundhouse until her retirement in 1965. She and her sister Helen Beisner were first employed as engine cleaners.

North Platte was one of the few points in the United States that employed women to operate turntables. When Union Pacific remodeled the roundhouse in 1950 and installed the new turntable, Catherine (Katie) Deidel, Florence Williams and Dollie McEntire took turns operating it on eight-hour shifts. When Katie was interviewed by the North Platte Telegraph she said, "It's not difficult. It's really very simple."

According to a 1950s article in the *North Platte Telegraph*:

"Mrs. Deidel thoroughly enjoys her work, though admitting it has its disadvantages. The little control booth, from which Mrs. Deidel operates the turntable contains two electric heaters. But two of the control levers extend through the floor and wintry drafts 'are downright chilling'. Blizzards are a real problem for the operator. Mrs. Deidel recalls that during the 1949 and early 1950 blizzards, vision was so limited that she couldn't see to line up the turntable tracks with those leading into the roundhouse. A second person was used to give the signal when the tracks were aligned. Cold weather also brings the hazard of steam, Mrs. Deidel points out. Though she walks in front of the locomotive as it enters the roundhouse, the engineer sometimes is unable to see her and she has to shout the signal that all is clear. All in all, Mrs. Deidel maintains, her job is a simple one, but she finds it fascinating to be working side by side with the men who are part of the huge railroading industry."

Katie's granddaughters remember visiting their grandmother at work:

Dolores Fraser says, "I helped pack her lunch pail and Katie gave me rides on the turntable."

Katie Deidel (1940s photo courtesy of Marjorie Taylor)

Sheryl Reinke adds, "I visited her at the yard. I got to go with her when she picked up her check but I was always scared crossing the tracks to get to the roundhouse."

Reminiscing about Katie, Judy Paul said, "Katie was a good ol' gal who loved to go dancing at the Eagles and have fun. She retired because she could make more money 'double-dipping' with railroad retirement plus social security.

She wore her hair up in a kerchief and never had any trouble with the guys. She used to say, 'I did this job when they weren't here and they're not going to give me a hard time about it now.'

One time Katie was mad and I heard her carrying on about problems she was having with the hostlers. I misunderstood and thought she said hustlers so when someone asked me what Katie did, I told them she was the Boss of the Hustlers. Katie loved laughing about that."

Katie died in 1978 at age 74. She is buried in Floral Lawns.

Store Department Workers

Maude Agnes Miller Campbell Hall Shaw

The war also provided an opportunity for Maude Agnes Miller Campbell Shaw. Maude was in her early twenties when she hired on to help in the Yard in 1917. At that time she was married to Union Pacific switchmen William Arthur Campbell. Her father C. P. (Charles Peter) Miller also worked for the railroad and her brother Bill Miller was in charge of one of the districts. They were a railroading family. After the war ended, Maude quit her job to raise her seven children.

Maude returned to work for the railroad in 1942 during WWII. Her husband William was killed in an airplane accident in 1924. She married a man named Hall and had an eighth child. That marriage ended and she married Henry Shaw. He died in 1938. In order to support her family—and contribute again to another war effort—Maude went back to work with Union Pacific.

When Maude came back to work during WWII, she and her daughter Dorothy Campbell Davis were two of the first ten women hired to take the place of the men going to war. Maude ran the turntable and cleaned the women's shack. Dorothy worked as an engine cleaner.

Maude Shaw died in 1970. She is buried in the North Platte Cemetery.

Genevieve Jeffers Easton

Genevieve "Jeff" Jeffers was one of those 100,000 women who was employed in a railroad job in the United States during WWI. Genevieve turned 16 in November of 1917. She quit school to help support the family and to help with the war effort. Union Pacific hired her as an assistant storeworker with her father Thomas Jeffers who was in charge of the storeroom. In 1920 Genevieve married William "Ike" Easton, a Union Pacific switchman, and quit to raise a family. Three women from Genevieve's family: two granddaughters—Patty Morris Smith and Kim Easton Oltman, and one great granddaughter, Christy Miller followed in her footsteps to work at Union Pacific. (* See page 114)

Mary Easton Hunt writes about her mother:

"Mom was the oldest of 12 children. From listening to Mom's stories she was a very obedient and quiet older child. Her father was very strict and her mother full of spirit. She often stated she was fearful of causing any

Maude Campbell Shaw worked during both World Wars (1940s photo courtesy of Marjorie Taylor)

Cousins Katie Deidel and Genevieve Jeffers (photo courtesy of Mary Hunt)

sort of commotion. She sort of quietly watched all the rest while of course almost raising the younger children as Grandma was ill a lot.

"The family had its good and tough times as all, but Grandpa Jeffers was a very proud man and according to Mom if one of the children got into a scrape he was there at the school or wherever needed to make sure all was taken care of.

"Mom met Dad when they were young and although she didn't think much about him at first, he definitely had eyes for her. They would have to sneak and meet because the Eastons were not quite good enough for Grandpa Jeffers approval. Mom saw a very good, kind, and gentle person in Ike Easton and knew he was for her. Even though she didn't have her father's approval she married the man she loved.

"Mom had to have a wonderful nature to go through all the hard times. She tells of living with her mother-in-law and loving her dearly. She says her mother-in-law taught her many things. Mom talked about taking her oldest kids in the buggy across the prairie to her mother's to help her as she was still having babies.

"Mom got along with everyone. She never worked outside the home after getting married, but worked hard making bread, soap, and helping everyone else. I think Mom had the most wonderful witty sense of humor anyone could have. She always came up with something funny to say.

"I can without any doubt say she was the strongest woman alive, as far as her spirit. She had the faith to move mountains and prayed for her children and family. She loved unconditionally and had an excuse for all or any mistakes made by kids and grandkids. I could tell Mom anything and have her understand my pain. She loved life, family and friends, Saint Jude and her rosary."

Genevieve died March 24, 1993 and is buried in the North Platte Cemetery.

Margaret Gleeson

Margaret was employed as a store helper for UP in 1919.

Ethel A. Frye

Ethel was both a secretary and a storekeeper for Union Pacific during WWI. In 1923 she became a bookkeeper for Dickey Cream Company.

Stenographers

Beulah McGraw Kiehm

Beulah worked as a stenographer from 1917 to 1929. In 1939 she married Louis Kiehm and moved to Cheyenne.

Pansy L. Davis

Pansy L. Davis, born in 1898, was a stenographer for Union Pacific in 1917.

Jessie Babbitt

Jessie worked as a stenographer in 1919.

Dorothy C. Hinman

Dorothy was a stenographer in 1919-20.

Minerva McWilliams

Minerva was employed as a stenographer in 1919. In 1923 she became the deputy clerk of the district court. She died in 1946.

Peryle A. Hunter Merrill

Peryle was born in 1900. She worked as a stenographer at the freight house for Union Pacific from 1921 to 1927. She died in 1968.

Elmyra W. Brodbeck

Elmyra was a stenographer in the depot in 1925.

Timekeeper

Vanita M. Hayes

    Vanita was a timekeeper in 1923.

Clerks

Jessie Joy Baker Hughes Estermann

    Jessie was born in 1899. She was a clerk in 1919 and 1920. In 1921 she married Thomas Hughes and became a manager for Western Union. She died in 1985.

Marion Isabelle Faulkner Birk

    Marion was born in 1899. She was a clerk in 1919. In 1920 she married Arthur Birk. She died in 1968 and is buried in the North Platte Cemetery.

Mary Elias George

    Mary was employed as a car clerk in 1919.

Blanch M. Fonda

    Blanch became a clerk for UP in 1919.

Louise Ottenstein Halligan

    Louise became a clerk for the railroad in 1919. In 1920 she married Vic Halligan, a football star for Nebraska. Louise died in Brussels in a car accident.

Mary L. Schlientz

    Mary was a clerk at Union Pacific in 1919.

Esther Schwaiger

    Esther was a clerk at Union Pacific. In 1925 she changed occupations and became a teacher.

The first Union Pacific Depot and Hotel was built in 1869 and burned in 1915 (photo courtesy of Kaycee Anderson)

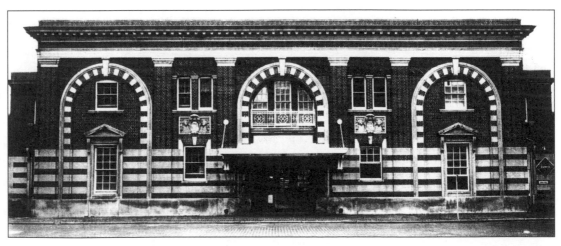

The Union Pacific Depot was rebuilt in 1917 and torn down in 1973 (photo courtesy of Kaycee Anderson)

The Women of World War II to 1960

Introduction

Women of the 1940s were pretty much homebodies. Most didn't question the role of barefoot, pregnant inhabitant of the kitchen. The government, however, needing more bodies in the workforce to replace the men it was sending off to fight, opened the kitchen door. Aiming to entice women to fill the men's positions, the Office of War Information developed what it called the Basic Program Plan for Womanpower. The plan included this strategy:

"These jobs will have to be glorified as a patriotic war service if American women are to be persuaded to take them and stick to them. Their importance to a nation engaged in total war must be convincingly presented."

And so began a propaganda blitz. Motion pictures, newspapers, radio, museums, employee publications, and in-store displays were all involved. Some 125 million advertisements were produced as posters and full-page magazine ads.

The government's war-related "get-women-to-work" campaigning was successful. At the end of December 1941, there were about 13 million women at work. Rosie the Riveter and other campaigns helped to increase that number to 15 million in early 1943. By 1944 there were 20 million women in the workforce, 6 million of them working in factories.

Railroading women were featured in *Click Magazine* in October 1943:

"Nearly 100,000 women, from messengers age 16 to seasoned railroaders from 55 to 65, are keeping America's wartime trains rolling.

"Women already comprise about 8 per cent of the country's total of rail workers. Next year may see 200,000 in offices, depots and yards. Twice the number so employed during WWI.

"What attracts these women to railroading? Some want the good pay which in 1942 averages $2,306 a year. Many are actuated by patriotism. Whatever their reasons, all are proud to bursting of the veteran railroaders' high praise: 'Ladies, you're doin' all right'."

Article provided by OldMagazineArticles.com.

During the war years, Union Pacific in North Platte hired women as engine cleaners, clerks, helpers in the store department and laborers in the car department. Women telegraphers, PBX operators and dispatchers made themselves at home in the communications area of the depot.

After the war, many of these women were willing to return to their kitchens, but many were not. Perhaps the government, as governments are wont to do, neglected to consider the ramifications of the program they developed.

Working outside the home was not for every woman, but the freedom to decide for herself whether to be a homemaker or wage-earner was liberating and exhilarating. Once women tasted the exotic dish of choice, they wished to continue to be free to choose. The media blitz to entice women into the work force for patriotic reasons brought about a discovery of independence that began the fight for equal rights and equal pay.

I grew up like a neglected weed -- ignorant of liberty, having no experience of it.
-- Harriet Tubman

Firemen / Oilers

Marjorie Hartford Halverson Taylor

In 1943 Marjorie Hartford lived with her parents on a farm in Boone County, Nebraska. It was not the most exciting place for a young girl of 19 to be and when her cousin Katherine Slattery wrote to tell her that Union Pacific was hiring women in North Platte, she packed up and took off for an adventure.

"You got to leave home sometime," she says, "I loved the farm but in the 1940s you didn't go many places. My folks wouldn't let me date and I didn't have a car to get to town. After I moved I was pretty homesick though, I can tell you.

"It was really a change from farm work to the railroad. First, all the clothes like long johns and high boots I had never worn, but I got used to them. You had to dress just like the men do and then you had a bandana on. All the women had to wear bandanas. We tied them up in front. My cousin told me to go shopping and get men's clothes before I came. You had to dress warm because the wind went right through that roundhouse. I liked it all right but too many men to suit me. I'd rather work around women.

"One of the things we did was clean the roundhouse of grease and parts or anything left by the men working on the engines. The men used cakes of dope to oil the rods and sometimes they threw them on the floor.

Marjorie Hartford (now Taylor) (1940s photo courtesy of Marjorie Taylor)

"Some days we washed windows in the cabs of the old steamers. Some days we cleaned engines. Two of us sit in a little shack waiting for the engines to roll up. The engineer pulls up and stops. He takes off and that's when we come in. We go out there and wash it. If two engines came in at once it was dark between them. We were supposed to wash the rods so the men could work on them without too much slop. It was a little shock to see how big they were. It was hard to get the inside parts that we couldn't see so well. They probably had some dirty engines when they got them in the roundhouse.

"Some days we were part of the Tank Gang and we washed the back of the engines and the tank. We used oakite and big long brushes. We rinsed them down with hot water from hoses. It took fifteen to thirty minutes to wash an engine. I can't remember more than that. It's been 50 years ago. More than that.

"I came from the farm. I thought this was play. You worked eight hours and you were done. We had coffee at 10 o'clock for an hour and an hour for lunch. At first it seemed like we were sitting around too much, but if we had two wash jobs at once it was hard to keep up.

"The shack is where the women collect. There are two rooms. One has a table and there was plenty of room to get around it. The showers and bathroom are over in the other room. The women eat their lunch there or they can take a bath when they get through working and change clothes.

"When I was working there I was thinking, *Wouldn't it be nice to go everywhere and work in every place and know as much as you find out there?* My uncle let me go in an engine, in the firebox, and see what was in there. I was so curious. This was one that was completely tore down. It didn't even have an engine on it. I went in there and there was a whole bunch of little rods or something all put together and that's to fire it somehow. I was curious what was in that firebox and he let me go in there.

"Some of the women worked on the rip track—the other half of the railroad. This side is engines, and the rip track is wheels and all that stuff. It's kind of divided. The engines are over here and the rip track over there.

"There were women in the back shops too. That's where they tore those engines way down and the women cleaned those parts. I don't know much about the back shops. I never worked back there.

"At one time I was a front end painter. I used a spray gun. I painted the front ends of engines, spraying them silver-colored. You had to hold on with one hand and paint with the other hand. It was difficult to stay balanced and reach around to get the sides. I didn't like the painting. I didn't feel like I did a very good job. If I can't do a good job, I don't like to do it.

"Sometimes I worked the turntable, but I didn't like that much. You had to get the tracks exact! If you didn't have the rails lined up, you had an engine on the ground and the men had to come and get it back on the track.

"I worked 8 to 4 at first. I lived next to Margaret and Ben Slattery. Both of them worked on the railroad. Margaret was like my second mother. They looked after me like I belonged to them. You know that Gene Slattery that sold his shirt to raise money for the Canteen? Him and his dad would go down to Fairmont's and get ice cream every day and bring me a pint of ice cream. They piled it up. They didn't just shut the lid. They piled it up and the lid would be open. They'd bring me one of them every day.

"I was laid off once and went home to visit. As long as I went down to the railroad station at Primrose every day and signed my name, I got a portion of my pay.

Marjorie Hartford (now Taylor) (1940s photo courtesy of Marjorie Taylor)

"I bid the job to put the oil in the engine. There was one place on the inside and one on the outside. I crawled up on the platform with the oil and filled the outside one. We carried the oil up in whatever it was. It had to have a spout because we poured it right in the lubricator. I don't remember what we carried it in. They were big things too. I was used to working on the farm. It didn't bother me. The inside one was usually hot and spit oil at you. It was like a living, breathing creature.

"Before you oiled it, you went out and put a flag on. There's an electrician that works at the same time. Either him or me puts the flag up and it isn't taken down until both of us get done. These engines were going out when I oiled them. We were supposed to go over and get tools out of the trains that were coming in and put them on the ones going out. They seemed to be awful short of tools. I don't know what they did with them.

"Two honks meant the engine was going ahead and three meant it was backing backwards. We all had to take two shifts once in a while. We got paid 99 cents an hour and we had two days off. At the time we thought it was big wages.

"Our group was called firemen/oilers. The 9000 class locomotive appeared in Cheyenne while I was working in the roundhouse. We worked on steam engines just like the ones in Cody and Memorial Parks.

"Oiling was my last job. I ran into my husband and got married. He said, 'Quit.' He didn't have to say it twice. That was the end of the railroad."

Marjorie was fascinated by photography. She says, "Since I was knee high to a grasshopper, I took pictures. That was just part of me." While she was still on the farm, her dad let her raise chickens and spend the money she made however she wanted. She bought a Kodak Brownie box camera. Thanks to Marjorie, we have photos of many of the women who worked on the railroad from 1943 to 1947.

Marjorie married Richard Halverson in 1947. They had six children: William, Robert, Douglas, Michael, Rodney and Pamela. Robert and Michael followed in their mother's footsteps and work on the railroad. Richard died in 1987 and Marjorie married Wayne Taylor. They were married 16 1/2 years before he died. Now Marjorie lives in North Platte and enjoys her 13 grandchildren and about 20 great-grands.

Grace Smith Essley

"I don't know the exact date I started. It was '43 or '44. Of course that was during the war and it was advertised that they needed women. Most of the women were glad to go up there and hire out and help during the war. They thought they were doing their part and I guess they were. Probably older women thought more about it than me, being 18. There was rationing you know, sugar and all that, but I never seemed to really realize that. We had as much sugar as we needed. We didn't need any more sugar than what we got. I didn't feel the hardships. I was happy to help out with the railroad. I thought I was doing good.

"My sister Lola worked for the railroad. We worked in different areas. She was born in 1924 and I was born in 1926. She worked the wash rack with me some but we didn't always get along. It was better when she worked the turntable. I never worked on the turntable.

"The pressure hoses that we used were all hot water, real hot, hot, hot. I cried for two weeks when I was on the wash rack. That pressure in those hoses and my arms—I wasn't used to doing that and my arms and shoulders hurt so bad. I'd come home and cry I hurt so bad. For an 18 year-old I didn't weigh that much at that time, 120 pounds, maybe 125. That was a lot of

Grace Smith and Marjorie Hartford (now Taylor) (1940s photo courtesy of Marjorie Taylor)

pressure and hot, hot, big hoses. After two weeks I was toughened in and I didn't cry anymore. Of course we wore protective gear and heavy gloves. We had overalls on and we had bandanas on our hair. We were protected. I never got burnt or anything like that.

"We used safety belts when we cleaned the jacket or main cab. We had a catwalk up there to walk on. We hooked the belt to a rod up there that was connected to the engine. It was very stable. We weren't allowed up there unless we had the safety belt on.

"I cleaned the middle main pin on the engine in the roundhouse. There was a big pit that the engine ran over. Of course the engine had to cool off before we could do anything. I got down in the pit to clean that and the engine was over me. The engine doesn't move when you're there. It doesn't move at all. It's cooled down. It's just the idea that it's over you in this big pit. It was scary at first but then I got used to it and it was just kind of old hat, you know, like anything. You get used to your job and that's it. Of course that wasn't actually

my job. That was a double over job. The wash rack was actually my job.

"We had a shower and a place for us to clean up. I didn't get out much and talk to the girls. I worked and then when I was finished I went home. The same with the men. I didn't really get to know the men but they treated me with respect.

"I was 18 and only worked one year. I met my husband at a dance when he was home from the service. He didn't want me working on the railroad anymore and that was ok too because I loved him. Some stayed there. I think maybe the men did resent that to a certain extent because the women were taking men's jobs after the war but it was their job so they stayed with it. There might have been a deep resentment there. I never felt that because I wasn't there at that time but I can understand how that can happen.

"I loved my job. It was hard at first. After you get accustomed to it then you're ok. We were paid well and we were helping out the war effort. The job was hard but a woman just has to be tough to be able to carry on.

Grace Smith (1940s photo courtesy of Marjorie Taylor)

"It was work but it was exciting for me, especially at that age."

Grace is 84 and Marjorie Taylor just celebrated her 87th birthday. They were friends when they worked together in the 40s. Recently they got together and discussed old times.

Grace: I don't remember getting tired or sleepy. Do you remember getting tired or sleepy on those big 16 hour shifts?

Marjorie: No, but look how old we were. We couldn't do it now.

Grace: Oh well, we can't do anything now.

Dorothy Campbell Davis

Dorothy Campbell Davis was born in 1920 and will turn 92 March 26, 2012. She and her mother Maude Shaw were two of the first ten women hired during WWII.

"My husband went to the service and I had to go to work to make a living. I had a little girl. The railroad was hiring so my mother and I went over and signed up. There was only ten of us women that signed up that day. They didn't hire anymore for quite a while. The men were leaving there, see, and we were taking their jobs. This is what they had lined up for us: they had a bucket out here with water and they had the longest brush handle you ever seen. You know how high them roundhouse windows were? They wanted us to wash them windows. They'd never been washed since the day they built the building. We told them, 'No. If that's all you need us for, you don't need us.' That's not a railroad job. Would you do it? So we was all going to walk out. So then they found jobs for us. Right then and there.

"I got one job I didn't want, but I was down the line a little bit. Seniority you know. My mother was a little ahead. It's when you signed in, you know. Well, I got the men's restroom. You wouldn't like that. They had all the sinks in the middle there. The men come in and take off their clothes and undress right there while you're in there washing the sinks. I turned my head the other way so I wouldn't see them. I didn't like that part. Would you? In the men's restroom there are toilets and stuff you have to clean. That was one job.

"Then they put me where I had to clean down the floors because water's all over where they wash engines and stuff so somebody has to get down and do all that. The windows were open all the time in the winter and you had to wear lots of clothes. It was freezing cold. I got that job because somebody bumps you and you take

Dorothy Davis (1940s photo courtesy of Dorothy Davis)

whatever they don't want. I got cussed so many times because I was shooting the water down there where men were hiding to keep from working. I got cussed for doing that.

"Then I got promoted again and I went into the other part of the roundhouse. I was in the machine shops and then I went into the other part. That's where I cleaned the cab windows, the indicators, and inside the engine and the outside. I did all of that. I did everything they had there but run the turntable. My mother did that. She stayed with that all the time.

"I did something I shouldn't have done. I don't think we were supposed to be on the back of the engines but we got up there and had our pictures taken.

"I had two uncles that worked out there. I always walked from Second Street across. We'd cut through the tracks to work, this other girl and me. That worked real good. But coming out to go home one afternoon, my uncle's standing way over there and he's a'yelling at me. I didn't know what he said so I stopped. I stopped right there on the rail. He was telling us, 'Get the hell out of there.' They had a switch engine on the other end. We just stepped out in time or we'd both been killed. So the next day they had a meeting for us about this and told us we couldn't cut through any more. We had to go clear down to Willow Crossing and walk clear back up to the roundhouse. Nobody had any cars. We walked wintertime—summer wouldn't have been bad but wintertime was hard. We walked all the way to Willow Crossing and I lived all the way west on Second.

"I was married when I was seventeen and my daughter Sandy would have been five when I worked. My oldest sister kept care of my daughter while I was working.

"To clean the engines we had brushes and oakite. You know what that is? It's lye. You get it on you and it eats your clothes. You carried them big buckets of lye

Pauline Jones and Dorothy Davis (1940s photo courtesy of Marjorie Taylor)

down the railroad. We wore them boots that didn't fit your feet, rubber boots, you know. No shoes inside. Just the boots. They didn't fit my feet. Over those tracks all day long carrying that oakite and washing engines. The engines were clear down the whole rail. You had to get your numbers from the head deal. You had to write them down to know what trains you go to. What I didn't like about it was at night when they want you to work over. If they said they wanted you to work, you had to work. You don't like to go down those places alone at night because some of those guys just scare the devil out of you. So my uncle was working over there. He followed me and waited when I went up to clean the cab windows and stuff. He was nice about doing that.

"I'd never worked in a place with all the men before. Mom was outside. She was outside because she knew stuff from WWI when she worked in the round-house. She quit between WWI and WWII. That's when she had all us kids.

"My hours working on the railroad were morning eight am until afternoon four o'clock. The men were nice. There were good bosses. I didn't have no trouble with any of them. We got $50 a payday. It didn't pay much then. I belonged to the Firemen/Oilers Union.

"I had uncles that worked at the railroad at the time. I could see them as they came around but I never stopped to talk to them. When you're working you got to do what you're supposed to do and not visit.

"You go in the shack to change your clothes and to eat your lunch. I never carried much lunch so I could just eat and go right back.

"And the gloves! Them were the biggest ol' gloves! I couldn't hardly keep them on my hands to work with them. Big ol' things. For men, not for women. You're using what men have. Like those big ol' boots. They didn't fit my feet.

"We had black faces when we went home. We were black from all that dirt and soot and stuff over there. We tied our hair up with handkerchiefs, with scarves. You know how you tie your hair to keep it from getting all dirty? The pictures will show them on our heads. I wore men's overalls. I finally got a pair of shoes. You had to have stamps to get a pair of shoes during the war. You couldn't just go buy a pair of shoes without stamps. I did get a pair of boys' regular shoes to wear.

"After a while them guys got through kidding us with all their jokes. It kind of wore out because we were busy. I think to start out they were just trying to see what we would do. I enjoyed the job. I hated leaving the people, but I wanted to be with my husband. I quit and went to Texas to be close to my husband. He was in the service."

Helen Engleman Stearns

"I started work for Union Pacific in 1942 and worked there for three and a half years. Mostly I ran the turntable. It was real easy. I just sat in this tiny little building until it was time to take an engine on to the turntable and into the roundhouse. When an engine came in, I marked it on a board to keep track of it and put it in a stall. When the engine was ready to go out, I pulled it out onto the turntable and turned it in the right direction to get it on the right track.

"I lost an engine off the turntable once when the signals got confused. I worked the 11 to 8 shift and carried a flashlight for signaling the engine onto the turntable and into the roundhouse. When it was slow, my girlfriend and I would signal each other with our flashlights about meeting up later. I was signaling her when one of the engineers thought I meant to signal him to come on. He ended up in the turntable pit.

"One time a gal came in and she was feeling pretty good. She put the engines in the wrong boxes in the roundhouse. People were running all around looking for them.

"We threw chains in front of the wheel to stop the engine, but one time Art Keithly was coming in too fast and went through the roundhouse wall.

"We wore jeans or pants made of a flannel material.

"I remember a time when Dolly McEntire and Big Ruth Baker got into an argument about who was hired first. They both wanted to work the day shift and seniority made the difference. Dolly ended up winning the debate and was able to work first shift.

"I liked it working for the railroad. I quit when the war ended and the men came back and wanted their jobs. Helen Barnhill and I decided to go to San Francisco, which we did. I worked in the Federal Reserve Bank for a few years and then came back home to North Platte where I lived all of my adult life until my husband passed. Then I moved to Arkansas to live with my daughter."

Helen is now 87 and lives in Arkansas with her daughter Judy Davidson.

Gladys Kariger (photo courtesy of Joyce Kohler)

Gladys Kariger, Kathryn Kariger Smith and Bertha Kariger Daharsh

Gladys Kariger was born in 1897 in Johnson City, Kansas. Her parents moved to Broken Bow and then settled north of Wallace, where she grew up.

In 1920, she married George Kariger. They had five children: George, Kathryn, Bertha, Harvey and Theo Mae. They farmed in several communities before moving to Sutherland where their children attended school. After her husband's death, Gladys moved the family to North Platte and began working for the Union Pacific Railroad.

Gladys's daughter, Bertha Daharsh of Gothenburg, shared these memories of her mother:

"She worked there 22 years and 22 days. It was dirty, dirty work scrubbing those engines. Can you imagine standing out there in the bitter cold scrubbing? How she ever did that, I don't know. Sometimes the men were naughty to the women and made messes on purpose for them to clean up.

"She walked to work, blizzard or sunshine, and never missed a day. She had five of us kids to feed by herself. Before she got the railroad job she took in laundry and her knuckles would be cracked and bleeding from hanging clothes in the cold. All of us kids worked too or

Gladys Kariger (photo courtesy of Joyce Kohler)

we would have starved to death. My sister cooked for harvest crews and I started working in a cafe at age 10.

"I thought I was grown when I was 16 and I went to work on the railroad with my mother. I had no trouble getting hired and I was doing the same work that my mother was doing. We were scrubbing those dirty engines and boxcars down, you know. A gentleman came up to me about quitting time the second day and he said, 'We'd like to see you up at the office.' I thought, *Oh lord, I wasn't doing what I should be doing or doing it well enough.*

"I asked, 'What's the deal?'

"He said, 'We found out you're only 16 years old. We can't hire anybody under 18.'

"I said, 'It wasn't because I wasn't doing the job?'

"He said, 'Oh no, we'd love to keep you but the law says we can't.'

"So I got my exit papers. Sixteen wasn't old enough to work on the railroad, but it was old enough to get married and so I did.

"It was several months after that—well, it was probably a year or more—that I got a check from them for a dollar twenty-one cents. I still don't understand. They said they didn't pay me enough and I had that

coming. I put it in a cookie jar because I was pregnant and I was keeping all my change. I was going to use the change to pay for my hospital bill when the baby was

Kathryn Kariger (photo courtesy of Kathryn (Kariger) Smith)

Kathryn Kariger's Schwinn bicycle used to call crews (photo courtesy of Kathryn (Kariger) Smith)

born. I had enough coins in that cookie jar to pay for her and my hospital stay. She was in there 15 days because she was premature. It took that long for me to get her up to five pounds so I could bring her home and the cookie jar took care of it. The dollar twenty-one cents helped.

"But I just don't know how on earth my mother did that day in and day out. You know blizzard or whatever. I can still see her yet with those overalls and that

Gladys Kariger (photo courtesy of Kathryn Smith)

red cap on her head going out that back door walking over there. I just wonder how she did that and survived as many years as she did. That had to be a horrible job for a woman to do.

"Mom had cataracts removed when she was in her 60s. They wouldn't let her go back to work after that, but they didn't forget her. She got a letter from the Union Pacific on her 100th birthday and a couple of railroad officials went to visit her where she lived in Oregon with my sister."

Another of Gladys's daughters, Kathryn Smith of Albany, Oregon, also worked for Union Pacific, but longer than two days. She was hired in July of 1943:

"I began working as a crew caller. If a man had no phone and lived within two miles of the roundhouse, I was sent on my bicycle to call him to work. I biked from the roundhouse and made three to five trips a night. When I started, we worked seven days a week and had no holidays off. My first bike was a Schwinn with big tires but I wore that out and my uncle bought me another one. I wore that bicycle out too. I did that job for about a year and then I became assistant dispatcher.

"My mother approved of my working for the railroad since it was a job and paid good money. I wanted to quit and go out and work in the shipyards in California but I was frozen in North Platte. They told me that my job was important to national defense and I couldn't quit. And it was important—about 500 trains a day came through and there were also the troop trains. I sometimes went and passed out magazines to the soldiers and collected soldiers' names.

"I was 19 when I started and I quit in December 1945 because my boyfriend came back from service and we got married."

Gladys moved to Albany to live with Kathryn. She died there at age 101. The Union Pacific gave her a watch when she retired and Kathryn cherishes it.

Dollie M. McEntire

Dollie M. McEntire was born in 1892 in Jefferson, Texas. She hired out to the Union Pacific railroad in 1943 as a hostler attendant and retired in 1958.

Lori Clinch writes about her great-grandmother:

"They always told me I have Dollie McEntire's eyes. Growing up and hearing the stories of my great grandma, I sometimes feel that must be all I inherited from her.

"I whine when I have to shovel dirt, swing a hammer or anything else that I consider to be man's work.

Dollie McEntire (1940s photos courtesy of Marjorie Taylor)

Dollie did it tirelessly and without complaint and she did it for a living. During an era when most women didn't work outside of the home, Dollie not only worked as hard as a man, but she worked in what was then a man's world—the Union Pacific Railroad.

"North Platte, Nebraska was one of the few places that allowed women to operate turntables and Grandma hired on in 1943. She took turns operating the machinery in the roundhouse for eight-hour shifts. She alternated with the other women who held the position, Katie Deidel and Florence Williams.

"For those not in the know, a railway turntable is a device for turning railroad rolling stock. These were in wide use when steam locomotives were still utilized. Unlike today's engines, they could not run in reverse at top speed. The engines would be brought in on one track and then turned and lined up with the track and in the direction they needed to go.

"These turntables also would have a positive locking mechanism to prevent undesired rotation to align the bridge rails with the exit track. This must have required a lot of effort to operate, and the women who did it must have been determined as well as able to use brute force.

"Trains were lined up on the tracks before they were moved onto the turntable. There was a lock bar

that expanded itself and locked the two tracks together. Dollie would then set the brakes on the steam engine, and release the brake to move the turntable.

"One day while in the roundhouse, she saw a steam engine coming out of the roundhouse by itself. It wasn't lined up with a track and she knew it would go down into the pit. Dollie jumped up, turned the table around, lined tracks up and then went out to put the locking bar into place. She had her hand on the locking bar and was going to throw it to lock the tracks when the steam engine hit the tracks.

"The bar went forward and came back and hit her in the breast. She got the engine stopped but ended up losing her breast as a result. The railroad gave her a $25.00 savings bond as a reward for her valiant effort. But Dollie didn't complain. It was part of her job and she was glad to have it.

"She always talked loud because she was used to being around the steam engines. She would have her railroad friends over to her house to play pinochle and other card games. It was said that they could be heard all around the neighborhood—even when the windows were shut.

"Dollie had three children that she raised alone: Coy, June and Fred. She was a good mom who always put their needs before her own.

"Dollie developed diabetes in her later years and had to have her leg amputated. When my dad was young, he often stayed with her and helped to take care of her. She loved him and cared for him in return.

"She worked until she got too sick to work any longer. She died in 1960.

"They always said I have my grandma's eyes. I truly hope I inherited at least a little of her spirit as well."

Loretta Schnitker Baker Faught

Loretta (Lettie) Schnitker was born June 16, 1922. She graduated from St. Patrick's High School in 1940. She was first employed as a waitress at the Dixie Cafe. She began working for the Union Pacific when she was in her early twenties. In an interview in 2010 Lettie shared a bit about her job and her life:

"We started out cleaning windows on the trains and they were dirty! We used oakite and hoses of hot water to clean the grease off the engines and we did roundhouse cleaning. A lot of us smoked and I now have emphysema and have to use oxygen.

Goldie Johansen, Lettie Schnitker, Pauline Jones, Martha Johansen (1940s photo courtesy of Marjorie Taylor)

"We women worked together and we got along. We had a good time in my day.

"I grew up on a farm in Iowa. I had eight brothers and seven sisters. I was the tenth child. Joe was my oldest brother. He had Joe's Dine and Dance and I worked for him for a while too."

Lettie died March 16, 2011.

Alma McCulla, Leila Shinley (1940s photo courtesy of Marjorie Taylor)

Leila Shinley (1940s photo courtesy of Marjorie Taylor)

Leila Surber Shinley

Leila S. Surber was born December 2, 1902. She married Neil Shinley in 1922 and they had two boys. Neil was killed in a car accident in 1934. Their son Dwaine Shinley shared these memories of his mother:

"I was nine and Kenneth was eleven when my dad was killed in a car wreck. My mother worked at about any job after he died to take care of us boys and herself. We traveled around and did migrant work. We worked fruits and vegetables in Utah, Colorado and Idaho. That's how we made our living. Each of us boys would bring in $5 a day and that was a bunch of money back then.

"My mother went to work for the railroad when I went in the army. She told me that after Kenneth and me got out of the service she wouldn't be working there anymore. She wanted to give the veterans a chance to get back to work. She worked because anybody who could hold down a job during the war made it possible for another person to help win the war.

"I worked on the railroad both before and after I served in the army. I think the ladies that worked up there enjoyed it. It gave them a chance to help out during the war. They ran the turntable. My mother did oiling. It was a job and the railroad paid about as good as any place around the country."

Leila died in 1951 and is buried in Stockville, Nebraska.

Margaret E. Hassenstab Slattery

Margaret E. Hassenstab Slattery was born in 1895 at Campsville, Illinois. She grew up in Alliance, Nebraska then lived and attended school in Humphrey. The family moved to western Nebraska when Margaret was in her late teens. As a young woman during WWI she lived alone and "proved up" homesteads in Wyoming for her brother and herself while he was in the service. Margaret and her husband Ben lived on a farm in Deuel County with their four children. In 1943 they moved to North Platte and Margaret went to work for Union Pacific. She retired in 1969 when she was 74 and died in 1979 at age 83.

As well as working for the railroad, Margaret volunteered at the Canteen. Her son John (Gene) was the young boy who often auctioned the shirt off his back to raise money for the Canteen. About his mother Gene says, "My mother was a strong woman with a pioneering spirit at a time in history when it was not always popular for women to display these traits. That explains why she applied for work on the railroad when it was not customary for women to work in jobs usually known as 'men's work'."

Gene's wife Anne says Margaret worked until she was in her 70s, always claiming she was only 65.

Margaret's daughter Evelyn Kleinau remembers her fondly. "She was a sweetheart; she really was. She worked hard."

Margaret Slattery (1940s photo courtesy of Joyce Kohler)

Katie Deidel, Helen Beisner, Frances Miller, Jessie Stephens, Gladys Kariger, Margaret Slattery, Tillie Sands
(1950s photo courtesy of Joyce Kohler)

Margaret's granddaughter Joyce Kohler described Margaret as a woman's woman. "She was a woman ahead of her time. She always encouraged me, often telling me, 'You've got to go to college. You've got to get an education.' I took trips with her on the train. We'd go to Wyoming to see her sister and to Humphrey where her family was from. She loved oatmeal and made our breakfast in the mail train using canned milk and hot water. She loved avocados too. She lived in an apartment across the street from where the State Theater was and walked everywhere. She never drove. Religion was important to her and we always walked together to church."

Margaret is buried in the North Platte Cemetery.

Mary Amelia Flynn Snyder

Mary Amelia Flynn was born in North Platte in 1884. She married at age 21 and had five children by age 27. In 1920 Mary worked as a census enumerator. In the 1940s Mary was almost 60 and her niece Gretchen Flynn thinks she probably went to work at the railroad as part of the war effort.

Mary Snyder, Goldie Johansen
(1940s photo courtesy of Marjorie Taylor)

Marjorie Taylor remembers Mary as a very friendly woman who cleaned the women's shack. "She was very particular and it was such an old building. She always wore blue coveralls—and she cleaned that old shack until it shined."

Mary's father James Flynn was an engineer for Union Pacific, her husband Ray Snyder was a conductor, and her son Austen Snyder was a superintendent. Austen had his own train car at North Platte.

A lifelong resident of North Platte, Mary was active in civic affairs and was secretary of the school board for several years.

Mary died in 1972 at age 88 and is buried in the North Platte Cemetery.

Helen Marcella Tatom Beisner

Helen Marcella Tatom was born in 1899 and died in 1958 at age 58. She and her sister Catherine Deidel worked together in the Union Pacific yards, both continuing into the 1950s after the men came back from the war.

She is buried in the North Platte Cemetery.

Goldie and Martha Johansen (1940s photo courtesy of Marjorie Taylor)

Helen Beisner (1940s photo courtesy of Marjorie Taylor)

Goldie M. Johansen Lum and Martha L. Johansen Merrell

Goldie M. Johansen was born in 1914 on a farm near Minden and came to North Platte in the early 1930s. After working for Union Pacific in the 1940s, she was a clerk at Montgomery Wards for 25 years. She married Bud (Irvin) Lum in 1955. She died at age 69 in 1984 and is buried in the North Platte Cemetery.

Martha L. Johansen, Goldie's sister, was born in 1916. In 1938 she was a waitress in the Lemon Cafe. She also worked for Union Pacific in the 40s. Later she was employed by Ludke Cleaners and then Memorial Hospital. She married Kenneth W. Merrell in 1968. She died in 1986 and is buried in Floral Lawns Memorial Gardens.

Dorothy Johanson (1940s photo courtesy of Marjorie Taylor)

Dorothy Johanson

In researching history, there's always just a little more to be uncovered. In the case of Dorothy Johanson, a little would be a lot more than the researchers found. Any information about her identity would be welcomed.

Johanna C. Johnson

Johanna C. Johnson was born in 1891. She was in her fifties when she worked for the railroad during WWII.

Goldie and Martha Johansen, Pauline Jones (1940s photo courtesy of Marjorie Taylor)

Johanna Johnson (1940s photo courtesy of Marjorie Taylor)

Pauline Jones

Pauline Jones was born February 22, 1910 and is now deceased. Pauline worked in the roundhouse. Her husband was killed in an airplane accident. Her sister Charlotte may also have worked for Union Pacific.

Zelma Kirts

Zelma Kirts's son Dale was about seven when Zelma worked for Union Pacific in the 1940s.

Matilda M. Frake Sands

Tillie Frake was born in 1897 and married William Sands in 1916.

According to the Polks City Directory at the North Platte Library, Tillie Sands (Mrs. Matilda M Sands) worked as an egg candler at Stensvad Poultry in 1942. Photos taken by Marjorie Taylor in the 40s indicate she was later employed by Union Pacific. Marjorie says Tillie worked in the back shops. A photograph donated by Margaret Slattery's granddaughter Joyce Kohler shows her as still employed at the railroad in the 1950s.

Johanna Johnson (1940s photo courtesy of Marjorie Taylor)

Helen Beisner (1940s photo courtesy of Marjorie Taylor)

Johanna Johnson, Pauline Jones (1940s photo courtesy of Marjorie Taylor)

Tillie Sands (1940s photo courtesy of Marjorie Taylor)

Zelma Kirts, Johanna Johnson, unknown, Helen Beisner, Frances Miller, Grace Smith, unknown, Gladys Kariger (1940s photo courtesy of Marjorie Taylor)

Helen Beisner (1940s photo courtesy of Marjorie Taylor)

Unknown, Maude Shaw, Elsie Cline (1940s photo courtesy of Marjorie Taylor)

Jessie Stephens, Tillie Sands, unknown, Dorothy Davis, Mary Snyder, unknown, Pauline Jones, Katie Deidel, Martha Johansen, Goldie Johansen, Helen Beisner (1940s photo courtesy of Marjorie Taylor)

The last entry for her in the Directory lists her as an engine cleaner in 1960. She was not only one of the first to explore new opportunities for women at Union Pacific in North Platte but also one of the courageous ones who continued to work after the war was over and the pressure to give up "a man's job" increased.

Alma McCulla

Alma McCulla is the woman on the right but no information could be found about her. Even the name of the woman on the left is unknown but it appears she enjoyed working for Union Pacific.

Unknown, Alma McCulla (1940s photo courtesy of Marjorie Taylor)

Jessie Stephens

Jessie Stephens moved to North Platte from Gandy, Nebraska and was hired by Union Pacific in the 1940s. She continued to work in the back shops after the war was over and into the 1950s. Her niece Mary Ann Blackledge says Jessie dressed as a man and called herself Jack so no one would bother her.

Bob Lowe remembers Jessie well. "She had gray hair and wore a cap kind of cocked on her head. Nice lady. She hired me to sell some vacant lots for her."

Jessie died in 1960 and is buried in McCain Cemetery between Arnold and Stapleton.

Ilene Hensley, Bess Naude and Elsie C. Cline

Ilene Hensley, Bess Naude and Elsie E. Cline all worked as engine cleaners in the 1940s.

Elsie E. Cline was born July 3, 1895 in Pittsburg, Kansas and came to North Platte in 1916 from Great Bend, Kansas. She died in 1967 at age 71.

Ilene Hensley, Bess Naude, Elsie Cline (1940s (photo courtesy of Marjorie Taylor)

Hazel Hultquist, Ruth Ogborn Larson Baker and Lola Smith

Hazel Jeanette Spencer was born in 1899 in Wymore, Nebraska. She married Raymond Anthony Hultquist in 1922 in Grainton. Hazel died in 1996.

Ruth Baker ran the turntable and was a fire knocker, the person who opened up the ash pans on the steam locomotives and knocked the live fires and ashes out. She was 6 foot 4 and was often called Big Ruth.

Lola Fay Smith worked in the back shops with Tillie Sands, Jessie Stephens and Zelma Kirtz. She also ran the turntable.

Florence Williams
(1940s photo courtesy
of Marjorie Taylor)

Florence Williams

Florence Williams was one of the women who worked eight-hour shifts on the turntable.

Hattie H. Gardner Dedmore

Hattie Gardner was born in 1894 to John and Ellen Gardner who traveled in a covered wagon to homestead near Farnam, Nebraska. In 1923 Hattie moved to North Platte. She worked for Union Pacific in the 40s. She was married to Harry Dedmore. She died in 1986 and is buried in the North Platte Cemetery.

Marilyn Gardner, a relative of hers in Farnam, said, "Hattie was a hardy, happy kind of a person. We always really liked her. She was fun to be around."

Marie Traudt Stone Kohl Brown

Marie Traudt Stone Kohl Brown was born in 1890 at Stockham and came to North Platte in 1920 after the death of her first husband Arthur Stone. She was employed by Union Pacific for nine years. Marie is buried in the North Platte Cemetery.

Katherine Hartford Slattery, Evelyn Beardsley and Ruth Motsinger

Katherine Hartford Slattery White was born in Pocatello ID. She was a waitress when she married George A. Slattery. She, Evelyn Beardsley and Evelyn's mother Ruth Motsinger, all worked as engine cleaners for the Union Pacific and all took turns running the turntable.

By 1950 Ruth had changed jobs and was a maid at the Pawnee Hotel. Katherine later moved to Richland, Washington where she died in 1973.

Martha Hazel Thompson

Martha was born in 1908. She worked as an oiler during WWII. Helen Stearns remembers one time that Martha was not paying close attention to her job. When the engineer came down from the cab, she oiled him instead of the train. Martha died in 1952 and is buried in the North Platte Cemetery.

Josephine Kovanda Kunc

Josephine Kovanda was a coach cleaner. Josephine married Melvin Kunc. She died in 1956.

Viola Atteberry Halsey

Viola was born in 1912. She worked in the roundhouse and was also an Army nurse. She died in 1996 and is buried in the North Platte Cemetery.

Viola White

Viola White worked on the rip track during the 1940s.

Evelyn Beardsley, Katherine Slattery in the turntable shack (1940s photo courtesy of Marjorie Taylor)

Gladys Kariger cleaning with Oakite (photo courtesy of Joyce Kohler)

There are many factors to be considered in cleaning passenger, kitchen, dining, baggage and mail car exteriors. On one hand, the amount of the soil to be removed must be taken into account. Its thickness, ranging from light road bed dust to bug juice and tenacious traffic film, helps to determine the material concentration and soaking time. On the other hand, the kind of soil (clay, sand, iron content etc.), is effected by such factors as the type of locomotive power and where it travels. Diesel powered equipment gives off an oily carbonaceous film; steam-powered units, dry carbon-based soils; electrically driven equipment, metallic dust soils.

Not only do the nature and the amount of the soil require consideration, but their geographical source may have an important effect on the kind of cleaner needed to remove them. Some surfaces may not respond satisfactorily to all kinds of cleaning materials. Therefore it is most important to know exactly the kind and sensitivity of the surface under the soil. Besides that the frequency of the cleaning operation on the maintenance or shopping schedule, and the type of cleaning equipment and facilities available, further complicate exterior car washing.

Materials for Car Washing

Recognizing all the problems of cleaning car roofs and sides, the Oakite Research Laboratories developed Oakite Compound No. 88, Oakite Composition No. 77 and Oakite Composition No. 70 to meet the special requirements. These safe, effi-

Page 5

cient, economical cleaning materials are especially designed to help you speed up and simplify manual and mechanical methods of car washing.

Oakite Compound No. 88, one of the most widely used, assures successful cleaning results when applied manually or with mechanical car-washing equipment on a regularly scheduled cleaning program. Simply by varying certain steps in those procedures, Oakite Compound No. 88 more than adequately meets all the demands of light, medium-and heavy-duty exterior car washing. Oakite Composition No. 70 and Oakite Composition No. 77 are recommended for washing cars where the soil is predominantly of an oily nature, and, in many instances, for washing aluminum cars.

Features of Oakite Compound No. 88

Oakite Compound No. 88 is a gray-brown, free-flowing, powdered cleaning compound. It cleans by means of vigorous wetting and penetrating action combined with effective detergency, resulting in activity that breaks up clinging deposits, and produces clean, film-free surfaces by improving subsequent brush-rinse operations. Following are the features and big advantages you gain by using Oakite Compound No. 88 as recommended:

1. **Superior wetting ability which takes the detergent action under the soil to loosen it.**

2. **Detergency which is effective on ordinary surface soils, plus the penetrating action that softens tough oxidized soils.**

3. **Safety to painted, lacquered, varnished steel and other ferrous surfaces.**

4. **No objectionable fumes.**

5. **Easy to handle and use.**

6. **Long life for the cleaning solution because of its high resistance to killing action of oil and grease deposits.**

7. **Free-rinsing action which helps eliminate left-over streaks on windows, roofs and sides of cars.**

8. **Good foaming action.**

9. **Helps restore luster to surfaces where luster is hidden by soil.**

Page 6

10. **Complete solubility which prevents clogged nozzles, permitting even distribution of solution.**

11. **Thorough window cleaning action.**

12. **Works effectively even in hot weather; easy to remove.**

13. **Economy of use because low concentrations give effective cleaning work.**

14. **Contains only ingredients that clean; no inert materials.**

Good Results Manually

In the manual method of washing cars, the surfaces are first wet with water and then the Oakite Compound No. 88 cleaning solution is applied with long-handled brushes from the bottom up. After the solution has been allowed to penetrate and loosen the deposits, brush-rinsing the surfaces with the fountain brush follows to complete the removal of the soil.

Those two steps make up the simple fundamentals of effective car cleaning with Oakite Compound No. 88. The wetting, penetrating and detergent action of this effective Oakite car-cleaning material easily accomplish the difficult work of loosening and removing the soils. Water-wetting the surface, applying the solution and rinsing off both solution and loosened soils is all the operator has to do. If it is necessary to preclean certain areas which are heavily spotted with grease, oil and carbon, Oakite alkaline or solvent type materials, used as recommended by the Oakite Technical

Automatic brushing and rinsing of a Diesel. Before this operation, Oakite Compound No. 88 was automatically applied as the Diesel moved by. In the 1½ minutes it took to reach the brushes, the Oakite solution completely loosened the soils so they could be easily flushed away.

Pages from a 1940s manual about cleaning engines with Oakite. (Information courtesy of Chemtall)

Service Representative, quickly provide excellent results when used before applying Oakite Compound No. 88.

Good Results Mechanically

Where the mechanical brush and spray system is used for car washing, Oakite Compound No. 88 is applied in recommended solution strength through the spray risers. It has been found that best results are to be had when the solution-applying riser and mechanical spray-brush units are approximately 100 feet from each other. This gives the Oakite car washing solution time to penetrate and loosen the soils before going into the mechanical brush and sprays. Usually one pass through the Oakite Compound No. 88 solution sprays, scrub-in brushes and rinse brushes will result in excellent cleaning. The vigorous detergent action of Oakite Compound No. 88 does its work quickly, effectively and without damaging the paint, varnish or lacquer.

Cars which have accumulated a heavy coating of soil may have to make several passes through the mechanical brush system (or its equivalent in manual washing procedures) before the full luster of the car surfaces is restored. But once the soils are completely removed the Oakite way, each subsequent cleaning with Oakite Compound No. 88, performed on a regularly scheduled basis, should easily and quickly produce bright, clean surfaces.

Spray-Brush Method Too

This method is most often recommended for exterior car washing when facilities and track layout will not permit installation of mechanical-brushing and rinsing equipment. Basically this technique consists of the mechanical application of the Oakite cleaning solution, and manual brushing followed by rinsing with fountain brushes.

Special spray equipment needed may be built in the railroad shop. Other equipment needed consists of a solution holding tank and a small pump or compressed air tank. This equipment delivers the cleaning solution to a pair of standards equipped with specially placed nozzles. As the cars move along the track, all surfaces are thoroughly wet and

Page 8

Spraying on Oakite cleaning solution on car surface. After a short soak, soils are manually flushed away with fountain brushes. Excellent where one track is allotted to exterior cleaning, or where little car cleaning is done, or where automatic equipment is not practical. Shows big savings over bucket and brush methods.

scrubbed with the Oakite cleaning solution. Then the cars move on to be rinsed with fountain brushes. This method effects big time savings over the bucket and brush procedure; and teamed with Oakite car washing materials provides excellent cleaning results.

Safe Cleaning of Stainless Steel Cars

There is a special consideration to be made before deciding on the kind and amount of material to use for exterior cleaning of stainless steel cars. The continued use and indiscriminate use of some commercial raw acids, for example, may cause corrosive attack on stainless steel. However, the special composition of Oakite materials recommended for this work provide a dependable safety factor. Oakite Compound No. 88 and other Oakite materials suggested by your Oakite Technical Service Representative have been thoroughly tested in the laboratory and in the field, and are free from damaging action when used as directed.

When there is a question about absolute safety in your car washing procedures, you are invited to call in the local Oakite Technical Service Representative or a representative of the Oakite Railway Service Division for consultation. In his suggestions to you, he will discuss recommended Oakite materials, the most effective solution concentration to use, various methods of application, the importance of controlling the soaking time between

Page 9

Cleaning with Oakite

In 1909 Oakley Chemical Company was founded with a product called Oakite, said to be a safe alternative to caustic soda and used for heavy-duty cleaning of artillery shells during World War I. Oakley Chemical Company became Chemtall.

Karen Sohl, a Chemtall manager, says this product is no longer made but in the 40s it would have been packaged in 55 gallon drums and 5 gallon pails. She shared a few pages from an old 1940s manual about how to clean engines with oakite.

Aerial view of roundhouse (1940s photo courtesy of Kaycee Anderson)

Side view of roundhouse (1940s photo courtesy of Marjorie Taylor)

Katie Deidel, Helen Beisner in turntable shack (1940s photo courtesy of Marjorie Taylor)

Pauline Jones, Katie Deidel at turntable (1940s photo courtesy of Marjorie Taylor)

Gladys Kariger, turntable, roundhouse (photo courtesy of Joyce Kohler)

Engine leaving roundhouse 1907 (photo courtesy of Kaycee Anderson)

Powering UP: A History of the Women of the Union Pacific in North Platte, Nebraska

Roundhouses and Turntables

A roundhouse is a circular or semi-circular building where engines are cleaned and repaired for their next run. Inside the roundhouse, tracks spread out fanwise like the spokes of a wheel. A turntable (a track pivoted at the center and supported at the ends by wheels which run on a circular track) sits at the base of the fan. Locomotives are driven onto the turntable track. The turntable revolves and the locomotive or railcar is moved onto a different track leading to an empty stall. When an engine is coming in, the turntable operator walks beside it. When it stops, she throws a chain under the wheel. Each stall has a pit beneath the tracks to permit inspection and repair of locomotives from underneath. When the locomotive is finished, the engine is driven back onto the turntable and the operator carefully lines it up with the tracks that return it to the yard.

Engine on turntable

In the past, turntables were used to turn steam locomotives around for return trips since their controls were often not configured for extended periods of running in reverse. They were also used to turn observation cars so that their windowed lounge ends faced toward the rear of the train.

North Platte's first roundhouse was built at the end of the 1860s and had ten stalls. A document sent from G. M. Dodge, chief engineer, to the treasurer of Union Pacific in 1868 states that the cost of the roundhouse was $80,000. It shows the cost of the turntable in North Platte was $1,500 and that $150,000 was spent for the shops.

In 1881 wind blew the roundhouse down and work began on a new one of cement with 20 stalls.

That roundhouse was replaced in 1913 with a 28-stall roundhouse.

In the 1950s the span of the turntable was increased from 100 to 126 feet in order to accommodate larger locomotives. The 3900s were 121 feet and 10 inches long and the 4000s were 132 feet and nine inches long. The roundhouse had handled the 3900s by jacking up the three rear wheels and suspending them but that was too difficult to do with the 4000s. The pit was enlarged as well when the 100 foot turntable was replaced. The remodel extended the roundhouse 25 feet and provided 23 stalls with all-glass walls.

This configuration existed until 1971 when the roundhouse, the powerhouse, and the machine shops were all razed to make way for a new $10.5 million diesel shop facility. Streamliner passenger service ended in 1971 also. Two years later in 1973, the depot and icing platforms were torn down.

It was natural for people familiar with dealing with horses for transportation to refer to locomotives as iron horses and to call the places in the roundhouse where they were kept stalls. The men who took them in and out of the stalls were of course called hostlers. The roundhouse is long gone and engines now go in one end of the diesel repair shop and out the other by means of switches, but those who move engines around the yard are still called hostlers.

Communications

Bonnie Pendergast McGovern

Bonnie Pendergast went to high school in Fonda, Iowa in 1942. A representative of Union Pacific came to her house after graduation to say it was her patriotic duty to keep our country going while the men were at war. They offered to send her to business school in Omaha for three months if she would promise to stay with Union Pacific for a year.

Bonnie McGovern in 2003 at the train display in Cody Park in the Hershey depot where she worked as a teenager. (photo courtesy of North Platte Telegraph*)*

Bonnie reminisces:

"I worked on the railroad from 1943 to 1945. I was a telegrapher. I went to Boyle's Business College for three months. They taught me telegraphy and typing. Well, I kind of knew typing, but not real good. Telegraphy was easy. I think I could still do it. I liked it.

"It was fun to get out and meet people. I didn't know where they were going to send me. I was hoping it was Wyoming. I wasn't a bit afraid. I couldn't wait to get going. I was just out of high school. I really didn't find anything hard about it.

"I went to work for the railroad because I didn't have anything else to do. I was just out of high school. I wanted to travel. All of a sudden a guy knocked on the door and my dad opened it. It was the guy from the UP. He said they were taking just one person from each town. If they took two from the same town, they usually didn't stay. They would go on back. Of course I knew I was going to stay. I wanted to go west real bad. I wanted to go to Wyoming.

"I went to Paxton, Nebraska. My first telegraph message was from a soldier stationed overseas to his wife in Paxton. That same day I handed up a message to a live, steam-breathing speeding locomotive while the station agent held on to me in case I got dizzy. He was nervous, but I didn't get nervous because I knew what I was doing. The trains would go by very fast. I just handed up the order hoop. I don't know, it never scared me. They'd just hold their arm out and take the message. The cinders—oh, they would get in my eyes terrible. In the morning I'd get more out of them. They gave me some eye-drops. One smart aleck guy said that I needed the eye-drops because I drank too much.

"Then I went to Archer, Wyoming. In Archer the only one there was the agent, his family and me. Then there was just nothing. I didn't want to stay there. I was bashful and I never said much. I did go to the grocery store in Cheyenne when the agent's wife went.

"I got called to Hershey and I ran the whole depot. My duties were taking telephone and telegraph messages, handing messages to trains and bookkeeping. I did the payroll for track maintenance crews every two weeks. I didn't want to stay there at Hershey. I wanted to go to North Platte.

"I bid into the yard office at North Platte and that was a real good place. The job at the yard office was to take orders from the dispatcher over headphones and then make at least 16 handwritten copies with a stencil and carbons. I stacked the orders for each train at the end of a long counter and the train crew would pick them up. I got bumped and I bid into the west end of North Platte.

"I just loved working on the railroad. I quit because I wanted to get married. I met Max McGovern the first day in North Platte. He was the crew dispatcher. They offered me any job I wanted if I'd stay, but Mac didn't want me to work. It was hard to give it up.

"I volunteered some days at the Canteen. One of the soldiers that came through was from Iowa and I'd met him at a dance. When I would watch the train go by a lot of the younger guys would hold out a paper and ask me for a date.

"I worked seven days a week. Everybody did. You were tired. About the only thing you did was work, work, work. The men were all gone to war so it was great for the women. Anywhere you wanted to be, they would put you there. Everything the women wanted the railroad would give us. The men didn't like that. According to the men, whatever the women got, the men should get more.

"Everything on the railroad was easy for me because I loved it. No matter what I had to do, it didn't bother me."

Mary Hunter Schaeffer

"I worked for the railroad midnight to eight mostly. I worked vacations for the other women. Actually I was scheduled one night a week, Friday nights. Then I only worked when somebody wanted off or somebody was on vacation.

"We were in a little room off to the side of the telegrapher's office in the depot. There were certain calls we had every morning, like every morning we had to set up for Grand Island, Cheyenne and Omaha. The dispatchers all talked to each other for a while about their business. Otherwise it was the little depots between Grand Island and North Platte. They'd call, but they weren't on the switchboard.

"I started about 1950. It was probably 1958 when I quit. We adopted our oldest son and we could not adopt if I was working. I probably worked right around 8 years. I don't remember now. I can't remember yesterday let alone now.

"I did many things I shouldn't have done. Like when the janitor went out the window to do something and I locked him out. It was like 20 below zero. He was hollering, 'Let me in.' So I let him in after a while. He was a good janitor.

"All of the telephone operators were women. I think there were five of us. Florence Stamp, Wilma Stack, Edna Brown, Margaret Griffith and me were there when I was there.

"There were at least two women that were telegraphers, Maxine Kosbau and Mildred Jergensen. I don't think there were any women in the other offices in the depot. There were some that worked out in the different offices away from the depot but we never saw them.

"One of the more challenging parts of my job was staying awake. I got off at 8 o'clock in the morning. I saw an awful lot of beautiful sunrises. It really was one of the best shifts I could work because my husband went to work at 2 o'clock in the morning. I went to work about 11:30. He would get off about 10 in the morning. It really wasn't a bad shift at all.

"Midnight to eight you could go an hour without a call. Of course people called each other and just talked because there was time then and they could do it, but you took care of company business first.

"You weren't supposed to listen in. You knew better than to say anything you heard. You might go out the door if you did because you weren't even supposed to be listening. There wasn't anything that great to hear anyway. The best one to listen to was the telephone operator up at Cheyenne. She talked about her boyfriends and how they dressed out a deer in the bathtub—things like that. She was a character. She'd talk about anything and everything. There wasn't any privacy to her.

"I would get off at midnight and a bunch of young boys would be walking down Front Street. They would spread out across the street trying to not let you through. I rolled the window down and I said, 'You have a choice. You can either get out of the way or I'll run into you because I'm not stopping.' They got out of the way. I slowed down but I said, 'I'm not stopping.' North Platte used to be very rough.

"We usually took two breaks during the night. One around 3 o'clock and one around 6 o'clock. Of course the North Platte Cafe was right across the street from the depot so we went over there and had coffee and talked and saw how the rest of the town lived. One night there was some doctors come in. This one doctor, he shouldn't have been out. He was telling everybody he was going to do surgery at 6 o'clock in the morning. I'm glad it wasn't me. You'd see a lot of that going on, what people did, because it was probably the only place open.

"There are things that I've forgotten and some of them I probably didn't know to begin with.

"We were just a bunch of normal people together. We thought we were normal anyway."

Mildred Majer Stacy Ickes

Mildred Majer was born in 1917, grew up and graduated in Ravenna. She worked at the Cornhusker Ordinance Depot in Grand Island during WWII. In 1943 she moved to North Platte to work for Union Pacific as a crew caller. She was an engine dispatcher when she retired in 1975.

Bonnie North enjoyed working with Millie. She said it always tickled her that Millie chained her chair to the desk every night so no one would sit in it. Millie was working downstairs in the general foreman's office at the diesel shop at the time.

Millie died in 2005 at the age of 88.

Lillian (Billie) Powell Guilliame and Evelyn Powell Gruball

Billie Guilliame hired out as a station agent and got transferred to being a telegrapher. She was employed from 1944 to 1946. Her husband Bob says, "She was the middle of six kids and she was a fighter. She just picked up telegraphy. Sending or receiving, one of the two, was hard for her. She quit because the guys were coming back from the Army and the Navy. She didn't like moving up and down the line either."

Billie's sister Evelyn also worked for Union Pacific as a telegrapher until she quit to be a telegrapher in the Navy.

Mildred Swift Jergensen

Mildred Swift was born in 1922. She met Dale Jergensen when she was a telegraph operator in Ogallala and he was a conductor. Dale is 93 and loves to talk about Mildred. "Her dad was a railroader. He taught her code so she could be a telegraper. She got so she could read the holes in the tape. One time when it snowed she couldn't drive to work so she rode a section car. She worked upstairs in the depot."

Her son Michael remembers:

"Mom talked about the hoops they used to hand messages to the engineers. She quit working when I was about three or four. The railroad was a good job for her. She lived in depots all the time she was growing up. Grandpa (Roscoe Swift) had fruit trees in Arkansas and then he went to telegraph school. He loaded the family and possessions in a boxcar and they all were taken to his first station. When I was a kid we went to visit him in Haig, west of Gering. There was a meat house and a potato shed for shipping. He was the last depot agent there. They closed it down when he retired.

"I remember visiting my grandpa. He lived in one end of the depot, the middle was the waiting area and had a pot-bellied stove and wooden benches. The next section was the office where the telegraph was and where business was conducted. It was where they sorted mail and sold stamps. The other end of the building was the freight room.

"Mom lived in a boxcar west of Laramie for a while. There were two boxcars: one was the depot and the other was for living. That's where she graduated from high school. She grew up in boxcars."

Mildred died in 2008.

Edna Gifford Moser Brown

Edna Gifford was born in 1914. She became a switchboard operator for Union Pacific in 1941 and was chief PBX operator when she retired in 1974.

Edna Brown's daughter Sharron Hewgley shares her memories of her mother:

"During the '49 blizzard Mom walked to work down 6th Street. When she got there, people were call-

Edna Brown in the office with her boss Vic Beloit in 1951 (photo courtesy of her daughter Sharron Hewgley)

ing in and saying they couldn't get to work. 'Well,' she said, 'Can you get to the tracks? They're running an engine up and down. If you can get to the tracks, ride the engine.'

"Someone called her and said, 'Who in the hell is telling these people to ride the engine?'

"She said, 'I am. Do you want them to stay home or do you want them to come to work?'

"She didn't hear anymore about it.

"April 15, 1963 was the worst day of her life. It was the day that guy killed people out at the freight office. It was around lunch time. Some of the wives of the men who were killed were at lunch and they heard it on the news. There was a news release before the next of kin was notified. Mom's switchboard lit up. She couldn't handle the volume of calls from the public and the officials and deal with the emergency calls too. She finally pulled all the plugs and told people to dial direct. There was an investigation. They said she couldn't have done anything else.

Sam Drummy called Mom to tell her to call the ambulances. That was when the ambulances were the hearses, too. She asked, 'How many?'

Edna Brown at the switchboard in 1951 (photo courtesy of her daughter Sharron Hewgley)

"'Send for all of them,' he said.

"There were three dead. That was her worst day on the railroad. She said she'd never forget it.

"She worked through World War II. In her later years she said, 'During the war, tires were rationed; sugar was rationed; people here felt it. We're at war now but it's like it's not even happening.'

"She was there the night the Canteen got its start. She went downstairs from her office in the depot. There sat the Rae Wilson family and many others she knew with big baskets of goodies expecting a train to come through with their sons, brothers and friends from North Platte. They finally figured out that they'd taken them through Kansas. They gave the baskets to another troop train. That's what started the Canteen. Thanks to everybody in North Platte and the surrounding towns it was a huge success. Over six million troops came through the North Platte Canteen.

"There were a lot of events Mom learned about first because they came through on the teletype. The day Kennedy was assassinated she called and told me about it before it was even on the news.

"She was a single mother and I was an only child. Because of her hours she claimed she raised me by telephone. I can remember Mom's schedule to this day: Monday and Tuesday she went to work from 4 to midnight; Wednesdays she had off; Thursdays were midnight to 8; Saturdays and Sundays she went 8 to 4. I was one of the first latchkey kids.

"Every Christmas we were just flooded with boxes of candy. Those guys appreciated the work she did. And she really liked her job. She always was grateful she had it."

Edna died in 2005 at age 90.

Maxine Lillian Estes Kosbau

Maxine was born in 1924, the youngest of ten Estes children. After her graduation in Scottsbluff in 1942, she attended school in Omaha to learn Morse code and International code. Union Pacific hired her. She retired 41 years later in 1984.

Her daughter Lynn Dee Nielson said, "It was difficult for Mom working in a man's world. When she finished Morse code school she was offered a job in D.C. but she needed her mother's signature. Her mother wouldn't sign because she wanted her to stay closer to home. Union Pacific came to the school and hired her because of her good scores. She was a telegrapher in a locked office with a lot of security and worked with all men.

"When I was in grade school and junior high, Mom was head ticket agent downstairs in the depot.

"She copied train orders to give to engineers. She had a headset. She could type the verbal orders as fast as they could speak. It had to be letter perfect—transpose a letter and you could have a train wreck."

Maxine died in 2000 at age 76.

Wilma Frances Stack

Wilma Frances Stack was born in 1916. In 1934 she graduated from St. Patrick's High School. When she was 26, she became a PBX operator for the railroad. She worked with Edna Moser Brown and Edna's daughter remembers Wilma as a woman who loved purple. She said Wilma always wore something purple along with heels and gloves to work. In 1969, after 27 years with Union Pacific, Wilma retired due to disability. She died in 1979 at the age of 63.

Margaret Carothers Griffith

Margaret was born March 14, 1912. She grew up in Maxwell and married Ray Griffith in 1931. In 1951 she was hired by Union Pacific as a PBX operator and retired in 1973. Carlene Griffith of Elephant Butte, NM writes about her mother:

"In the beginning Margaret worked only one day a week from midnight to 8 A.M. She also was available to work if one of the other operators wanted to take time off.

"The office was located in the upper level of the depot downtown. This building is now gone. The last few years Margaret reported to the office in the west end.

1960 photo of Wilma Stack, Billie McPeak, Margaret Griffith, Viola Thomsen, Edna Brown (photo courtesy of Sharon Hewgley)

"Other ladies in the office were: Florence Stamp (chief operator), Edna Brown, Wilma Stack, Billie McPeak and Viola Thomsen. After Florence retired, Margaret was able to work full time, first the midnight to 8 A.M. shift and later the swing shift. This was a perfect occupation for Margaret as she loved to talk on the phone."

Margaret retired after 22 years, 11 months and some days. She enjoyed sharing this information.

Billie J. McPeak

Billie was born in 1907. She married Carroll LeRoy McPeak in 1925. In 1938 she began work as a telegrapher in Laramie and retired as a PBX operator in North Platte in 1973 after 35 years with Union Pacific.

Billie's daughter Carol Wrede lives in Greeley and shared these memories of her mother:

"My father wasn't well. He died when I was 12. I grew up on trains. I was an only child, a 25th wedding anniversary surprise. I was conceived when my mother came back from the war effort. My mother was 42 and my father was 50 when I was born.

"When Mom began working in Laramie they still had wood burning and coal burning engines and an ice house. There weren't too many jobs for women without teaching or nursing training. She thought working for the railroad was wonderful and they treated her good.

"In North Platte she worked with Margaret Griffith and Viola Thomsen. She had all the cords for UP memorized and didn't have to look them up. She liked working nights when it was more casual.

"When I was in junior high, there was a conductor's strike and the telegraphers went off in sympathy but Mom wouldn't walk off the job because she needed the money. Sympathy strikers didn't get paid. She was inside when it began. She and another worker didn't leave the office for two weeks. They kept the trains going. She didn't have the money to strike. She needed to pay the rent, but there were a lot of hard feelings about it.

"She was a very outgoing person and a storyteller. She lived long enough to know her grandchildren.

"I have her 1947 union card and service pins. She was in the signal corps. She had life membership in the Old Timers Club.

"When they automated the PBX board she no longer had a job with the railroad.

"Women who worked then are to be commended. Those who stayed after the men came back from the war took a lot of heat and were not appreciated."

Billie died in 1997 when she was 90 years old. She is buried in the North Platte Cemetery.

Viola M. Schmidt Cool Thomsen

Viola Schmidt was born in 1925 in Blue Hill, Nebraska and moved to North Platte in 1940. She married Gene Cool in 1944. He died in 1957. In 1961 she became a telephone operator for Union Pacific. She married Henry Thomsen in 1970. In 1981 Viola retired after 20 years of service with Union Pacific.

Her sister Leora Prout says, "Viola was so grateful for her job. She'd been a diabetic since childhood and didn't know if they'd hire her. She could regulate her sugar by feeling but she always had to do the shots. She and Dr. Waltemath got diagnosed about the same time and they had lunch together once a week.

"Someone told her she should try to get that job because she had such a wonderful voice or she might never have thought about applying. She had a happy telephone voice and a string of friends—some of whom she only knew by voice. Viola was so proud of her gold pin for 20 years of service."

Her sister Pat Knudsen says, "She loved the UP calendars and always got them for herself and all the family. She bought both of us UP jackets. She made sure we saw where she worked and took us on a tour up to her office and later out to the new yard. She was always curious and knew a lot about the people she talked with. She could remember the details and ask them about their families."

Coleen Reutzel, Viola's stepdaughter, remembers that Viola loved her job and was very proud of being a UP employee.

Viola also participated in the Canteen during WWII. She died in 1989 at age 64.

Marilyn Maseberg

Marilyn Maseberg attended Russell Training School in Omaha in 1943 to learn telegraphy.

"Our teacher made sending Morse code on the wire seem easy. I didn't realize that out on the line there would be people sending messages who didn't pause between words. It sounded like one big mumble-jumble. I sweat, sweat, and sweat, and broke in again, again and again to have it repeated.

"I started at Rock River, Wyoming. I was to pick up consist lists thrown off the caboose by the conductor. Consist lists were sheets of paper wrapped around a rock and fastened with a rubber band so they would not blow away before I was able to rescue them. The first sheet was a summary of contents I was to relay to the dispatcher of the Green River yards. I was responsible to list every car and its contents. I was so slow and the ones I worked with were so patient. We usually had five or six switch lists on any eight-hour shift.

"We took Western Union wires too. One man always ran everything into one long word, without fail. Was he old and too tired to take his hand off the key? I never found out.

"A local came through on my shift. We always had several cans of cream plus lots of freight to load. There were several men who showed up to help me.

"New marching orders came two weeks later.

"'Next stop Buford,' the conductor called out. All I saw was gravel. No trees or grass. At 19 I was both scared and excited. I was expected to start work at midnight, but nobody was on hand to show me where anything was. Joe the engine turner helped more than he knew.

"We always started our eight-hour shift by giving the time. It was a while before I realized how important five minutes could be. It could mean safety or a real train wreck. We all carried our own watch and put it on a little nail just across from our eyes in front of us.

"Our main job was to OS (Out of Station) the trains as they went by. It let the dispatcher know where each train on his district was.

"The tracks in Buford were close enough together that we didn't dare stand between them if a train was due by from both directions.

"We had a headphone and a foot pedal we pushed down when we OS'd trains so our hands were free to take down train orders. We wrote train numbers in a book. The number was on the front of the engine in bright lights.

"If we had a train order, we put the red board out. Train orders (called "flimsies" because they were on such thin paper) were picked up before the crew left a terminal. Operators along the line used flimsies to relay any pertinent news once they were out on the line. We used a stick about three feet long that forked out on both sides to make a V. We made slipknots with twine so we could pull the message up tight once we inserted it between the knots. Both engine and caboose got messages. They slipped their arm through the triangle to detach the flimsy from the stick.

"The tunnels were a nightmare for the steam engines. They shut windows, covered their mouths, and tried not to breathe until they were in the fresh air on the other side. The cinders caused eye problems too. They stuck real bad in cold weather. One man carried a horsehair in his time book to scrape out the cinders. The horsehair acted like a fishhook.

"My home was a one-room shack with a single bed. There was a little stove but I had to haul the coal from behind the depot. I got water from inside the depot. There was one spigot and it ran cold. I used wooden boxes to make a table and stuffed a few things below. Otherwise, I lived out of my suitcase.

"The depot sat in a desolate area surrounded by deep gashes made from hauling out so much gravel. The commissary and a bunkhouse were down over the bank. Three section houses were east of me.

"The chief dispatcher sent girls out, one by one, to train with me on the midnight shift. They moved in a bunk bed and more blankets. Company was a commodity I sure enjoyed.

"Somebody sold me a bug for $5. This was an attachment to the old Morse key that made the key semi-automatic. One could send messages much faster once they learned how to use it. It was smoother and easier to 'read'. I practiced when I wasn't busy. I read that early operators sometimes used the key so much that their arm would freeze up. It was called Operator's Paralysis. They had to quit as their arm would never recover.

"Three of us lived in my 10x18 shack with the double bunk bed. The bunk bed did double duty. Years earlier telegraphers worked 12 hours shifts, and sometimes shared the same bed at the rooming house. If they asked to see the room before paying for the bed, they would be told somebody was sleeping in it. They were told sheets were washed once a week, but one wonders if they were. That would be a lot of laundry to do in one day without modern equipment nor a way to dry them. They had no indoor plumbing. You can imagine how often people had a bath or clean clothes.

"We wore clothes that would not get hooked easily by a train. Jeans were quite new in 1943. Girls were still wearing dresses. The wind seemed to blow at all times. The gravel pelted our legs through our jeans. We didn't have any facilities for washing heavy jeans. We didn't hang anything outside as the smoke and cinders and gravel could cancel out our clean clothes. I sent my laundry home to Mom. Spit baths were another norm for the hill.

"I bid the station agent job and got it. I managed to get through my monthly reports I sent to Omaha. Railway Express was used mostly by the Mexicans going back and forth to Mexico. We weighed and tagged the bedrolls when they left to go home. I got 10% of the money for handling it. There was a book on hand that showed me how to charge, and make out the reports.

"The trainmaster gave a demonstration on lighting a fusee. We took the cap off and struck it a certain way. We could swing it or stick it in the ground. It would not go out in any kind of weather. The trainmen never ignored a lighted fusee. They stopped for it just like they did for a red board.

"It snowed over a foot both Easter Sundays I was on the hill. I remember anchoring my feet in a snowdrift and handing up to a doubleheader passenger train. I could feel that engine's hot air breathing on me as it went by. I went inside and just sat down for a while to recover.

"I hated the 10 am yard check. Every station from Cheyenne to Rawlins had to give their yard check by Morse code.

One day Mr. Jones showed up and told me, 'You'll have to check inside each car to see how much is in it.'

"'You mean I have to climb that metal ladder on the side of each car? That will take all day, every day.'

"'The officials need to know the type of car, number of cars, how full each is, and how long they have been here for your 10 am yard check every morning.'

"No use thinking I would ever get anything else done but a yard check every day. I got up about 6 am to trot up to the yards a mile west. Yes, I climbed to the top and peered down inside every car.

"When we heard the good news of V-J Day in August, 1945, I sent my resignation in. Ms. Wood asked me to work another year until the fellows were back, but I had just celebrated my twenty-first birthday and was ready for indoor plumbing.

"We girls did a good job on the home front while our guys were off to war. We had a right to be proud of the job we did to keep men and supplies moving from coast to coast. We worked together well. I don't remember too many personality clashes. It probably helped that we were moved around often.

"I used my railroad savings for college. I was a secretary then I married and moved to the sandhills, a great place to raise eight children. I retired to North Platte and am still here."

Marianne Dolan Wallace Dunn

Marianne's daughter Jeanette Pappas writes about her mother:

"My mom worked for Union Pacific during the 40s, 50s and 60s. She retired with a full pension. She started work as ticket agent in the depot and later was a crew dispatcher in the roundhouse. Both buildings are gone and both were amazing. I remember going to the roundhouse. It had a dirt floor. There were different doors around the building so the engines could be moved to different tracks. My mom would let me go out there sometimes and watch. Now of course trains are broken up and reassembled on the hump. My mother's office had a wood floor and an old stove, but it was very dirty. The workings of the roundhouse created much dust and soot. Steambursts from the engines really blew it around.

"Once I saw an old man with a bucket and what appeared to be mop, only bigger, slopping water up on the engine. I looked harder and realized it was a woman. My mother told me that during the war when so many of the men were gone, women took over their jobs. This woman was a hang-on from then. This was how they cooled the engine down.

"Mom also told me that when she first started dispatching, not everyone had phones. They had runners to go tell men they were called for the next crew. She said even men who had phones were not always home so a runner would go find them. As everyone knew everyone else back then, they knew where they were likely to find them. Often this was their favorite bar.

"My mother was the only woman in that whole building as far as I know except for the old lady slopping down the engines and she soon retired. Back then there were no women engineers or conductors like now.

"Mom was hard-nosed and tuff; she didn't take any crap off any of the men she worked with so they respected her. She knew half the men in North Platte because they worked for the railroad. She also knew all the stories and gossip but didn't ever share. She said it was nobody else's business. Believe me, railroaders gossip. Or should I say MEN gossip. She worked nights for many years since there were only three dispatchers and three shifts. She finally worked her way to days."

Marianne died in 1990 at the age of 72.

Arlene Boggs Ricketts

Arlene Boggs attended the Emily Griffth Opportunity School in Denver to learn telegraphy. She was sent to work in Bitter Creek in 1944.

History of Communications

In 1844 Samuel Morse sent coded messages by electrical transmission over a wire. In 1846 Sarah G. Bagley became the first female to enter telegraphy as a profession. Sarah was contracted to run the telegraph office in Springfield, MA in 1847. Discovering she earned only three-quarters as much as the man she replaced, she quit.

In the 1850s railroads used the telegraph as a signaling device. Elizabeth Cogley was the first female operator to work for a railroad. After 44 years she retired with a monthly pension of $26.05.

During the Civil War (1861 to 1865), male telegraphers were drafted into the Military Telegraph Corps of the Union army. The hundreds of vacancies in civilian telegraph offices were filled by women telegraphers. They learned telegraphy as apprentices or attended telegraphy schools. At the Deseret Telegraph in Utah it was not unusual to find three generations of women operators who passed the skills along in the family.

When the war ended, many women were unwilling to give up their jobs. Some, having lost husbands, needed the jobs to survive. Others, having discovered life outside the home, resisted re-domestication. When a woman wrote a letter to the journal of the National Telegraphic Union to ask if women were allowed to join the union, the issues surrounding women working erupted in the pages of the *Telegrapher*. The responses illuminate the prejudices faced by women in the 1860s: women are less competent than men; it's unwomanly to be employed outside the home; and—contact with a man's world would contaminate woman's feminine goodness.

In 1861 the Pacific Telegraph Company of Nebraska constructed an overland telegraph line from Omaha to Salt Lake City. Operation of the Pony Express ceased two days after it was complete. This line was replaced in 1869 by the multi-line telegraph built alongside the route of the transcontinental railroad. As the last spike was pounded in at Promontory Point, a telegrapher matched the strikes of the hammer with his keystrokes on the new telegraph line.

In the 1870s Western Union recruited women and sent them to school free of charge. Though Western Union was motivated by the opportunity to lower operating costs (women worked for less money than men), they contributed to the number of women in a "high-technology" industry and more women began to work outside the home.

The Union Pacific Depot and Hotel in North Platte was constructed in 1869. It contained the telegraph office. When it burned down in 1915, a new depot was built. The telegraph office was located on the second floor along with the PBX (Private Branch Exchange) telephone switchboard.

Union Pacific encouraged women to go to school to learn telegraphy, particularly during WWII. Marilyn Maseberg writes in her autobiography:

"I want my children to know what the gals did while the railroads were running supplies and men across the continent through those years. We were hired because the young men were being taken to fight the war and nobody was left to fill their places. Finally Bill Jeffers, president of the Union Pacific Railroad and former North Platte boy, gave girls the 'go-ahead'.

"The Russell Training Service in Omaha handled my training class of 26 girls that summer of 1943. We were charged a fee of $50 which I found very hard to come up with. My mom, my sister and I all got our piggy banks out. We came from South Dakota, Nebraska, Iowa, and Waco, Texas. We were in school 12 weeks.

"We went to Cheyenne for our book of rules test. We had a list of places where they needed an operator on the line. Marjorie chose Granite Canyon. I got off at Rock River, and Dorothy went on to Walcott. Others went on west farther—some as far as Oregon."

Employees with telegraph duties sometimes handled Western Union telegrams. At small depots, they were often station agents and ticket clerks. The typical depot paralleled the railroad tracks. One end was a freight room with scales; the other end was a waiting room for passengers, usually with a pot-bellied, coal-burning stove for heat. The depot office was next to the passenger waiting room. Outhouses were about 25 yards from the depot.

Train orders (meet orders, wait orders, slow orders, orders pertaining to bad track or men working) were transmitted to the telegrapher who transcribed them onto flimsies—sheets of very thin paper because as many as seven carbon copies were made. These were "handed up" to the engineer at the front and the conductor at the rear of the passing train. At first flimsies were attached to five-foot-long bamboo poles with a hoop at the end. The operator stood close to the tracks and held up the order hoop. The trainman ran his arm through the hoop and pulled it out of the telegrapher's hand as the train sped past the station. He then tossed the hoop alongside the track.

Arm injuries occurred when the telegrapher was slow to let go of the hoop. Occasionally the telegrapher was jerked down on his back. The old train order hoop was replaced with the "Y" shaped train order stick. Now the telegrapher placed the order in a string threaded around the stick and attached by a slip knot. The trainman took only the string with the order.

When a semi-automatic transmitting key called the Vibroplex "Bug" machine was invented in 1904, more telegraphic traffic could be sent in an hour than one could send in a day with a key. The bug was based on a long horizontal lever that rotated around a vertical pivot. Pushing a paddle to the right caused a spring-mounted contact to vibrate against a stationary contact, making strings of dots. Dashes were made manually by pushing the lever to the left. The speed of the dots could be altered by sliding a weight along the lever.

There was some concern among telegraphers in 1876 when Alexander Graham Bell invented the telephone. The first telephones were rented in pairs and could only talk to each other. Soon came the central exchange and even small towns installed switchboards. In populated areas, switchboards were mounted floor to ceiling to accommodate all the lines. Ladders were used to reach the higher connections so limber young boys were hired. The boys' hijinks, high spirits and exuberance led to the hiring of women as operators instead.

In 1878 Emma Nutt became the world's first female telephone operator. Other women (carefully interviewed for assurance of docility, good character and long arms) followed. Telephone operating became a woman's profession.

Most railroads constructed their own internal telephone systems and train dispatchers used them to communicate train orders. During the 1920s PBX operators used a switchboard to connect a call by inserting a pair of phone plugs into the appropriate jacks. When the telephone receiver was lifted, a light came on above the jack. Each pair of plugs was part of a cord circuit. A switch allowed the operator to participate in the call. The earliest systems required a generator on the phone to be cranked by hand.

In his autobiography, *A Life with the Union Pacific*, Edd Bailey states: "These ladies were just like the telephone operators for Bell and were located in each terminal in the system. They were the main source of information for everyone along the line. All railroaders were required to check in with them if they were going to be away from phone contact for very long."

In the 1960s, the switchboard was phased out in favor of the automatic exchange, an early electric telephone line manager. The telegraph was gone by 1960. In the late 1980s Union Pacific closed the PBX office in North Platte and transferred it to Omaha.

After WWII, most major railroads installed CTC (Centralized Traffic Control) systems Using CTC a train dispatcher could align track switches. Trains could move into and out of sidings without stopping to hand throw switches. The train dispatcher also controlled the track-side signals. Satellite radios enabled train dispatchers to communicate directly with train and engine crews.

In March 25, 2002 Network World posted an article about one of Union Pacific's latest PBX developments: Calling from a train yard, a rail car supervisor can connect to Union Pacific's speech-recognition system with a request. The system converts the voice-based request coming through Union Pacific's PBX and converts this spoken information into Web text. The system then updates Union Pacific's Web server of rail car information. It also has a "voice biometrics" security feature that confirms the caller's voice using a digital voice sample stored in the speaker-verification database.

Morse Code

Technological innovations in radio, telephone, and computer have made Morse's messaging system obsolete but those interested in communicating with their index fingers instead of their thumbs can find instructions on the internet detailing how to make a telegraph. American Morse code, or Railroad Morse, has been almost completely replaced by International Morse code, but Chapter VIII Hints to Learners in the handbook, *Modern Practice of the Electric Telegraph* by Frank L. Pope, provides the basics of using the telegraph for communication:

150. Formation of the Morse Alphabet.--- The characters of the American Morse Alphabet are formed of three simple elementary signals, called the dot, the short dash and the long dash, separated by variable intervals or spaces. There are four spaces employed in this alphabet, viz., the space ordinarily used to separate the elements of a letter ; the space employed in what are termed the "spaced letters," which will be hereafter referred to ; the space separating the letters of a word ; and lastly, that separating the words themselves.

The value of these spaces should be carefully impressed upon the mind of the learner. Beginners are apt to conceive that the Morse alphabet consists solely of dots and dashes, and this misconception has a tendency to greatly increase the time required to become good "senders."

Uniformity and accuracy in spacing is of no less importance than in the formation of the letters themselves. The foundation of perfect Morse sending lies in the accurate division of time into multiples of some arbitrary unit.

151. the duration of a dot is the unit of length in this alphabet.

1. The short dash is equal to three dots.
2. The long dash is equal to six dots.
3. The ordinary space between the elements of a letter is equal to one dot.
4. The space employed in the "spaced letters" is equal to two dots.
5. The space between the letters of a word is equal to three dots.
6. The space between two words is equal to six dots.

The dot is an unfortunate appellation for this sign, because it conveys the idea of a point, or to speak electrically, a current of infinitely short duration. Electro-magnets, however, require time in magnetization (38). Currents involve time in transmitting signals. Clock-work requires time to run. Currents must be of sensible duration. The dot, therefore, involves time, but this time is variable, according to circumstances. The length of the dot should increase with the length of the circuit. In long submarine lines the dot has to be made longer than the dash itself on short open air lines, and the same thing occurs in working through repeaters (76). In commencing, therefore, the habit should be acquired of making short, firm dashes, instead of light, quick dots. After the student has once learned to send well, it is very easy to learn to send fast, but after once getting in the habit of sending short and rapid dots, or "clipping," it is almost impossible to get in the way of sending firmly and steadily. Beginners should rather take pride in the accuracy with which they space out the elements of the telegraphic music than in the number of words they can stumble through in a minute.

Taken from http://www.civilwarsignals.org/pdf/popebook.pdf.

Car Department

Thelma Hill Wilson

"I worked on the Union Pacific Railroad in the car department in 1943. I did not stay on after the war was over. It was a godsend to have a job there. My father was dying of cancer and my three brothers were all in service. We thanked the Lord the boys all lived through it. The ladies in our neighborhood had a prayer group who gathered once a month and prayed for each of their boys and made cookies and so forth. Each lady sent a box of goodies to their men and sons and, you know, every one they prayed for came home.

"My working made it possible for me to help my parents. My husband raised a big garden and shared it with them also. All three of my brothers sent home an allotment for my parents. We were all so grateful we were able to help them and that the railroad gave us ladies work.

"These are the ladies I recall who worked when I did: Mrs. Snyder kept the locker room spick-and-span. Dolly McEntire, Lettie Schnitker and Viola Atteberry Halsey worked in the roundhouse. Josephine Kavanda was a coach cleaner. Lena Flock Edwards, Frances Walters and Frances Miller were laborers in the car department. Maude Shaw and her daughter Dottie Davis washed engines. Pauline Jones—I think she worked in the roundhouse. Her husband was killed in an airplane. She was left with a little girl and was pregnant with another one when it happened.

"We went around picking up the scrap metal that the railroad men took off of the boxcars when they had to change the wheels. That stuff was really heavy. Sometimes two of us had to lift them to get them up in the truck. Once in a while they had a celebration over to the Jeffers Pavilion at the foot of the viaduct. We had to carry chunks of ice over there and put them in the icebox so they could have cold drinks for the people to buy when they danced and had a good time. That was the railroad that did that.

"Frances Miller would stop at my house and I'd finish taking her to work. We'd go right down Front Street in my car and we'd park right by the railroad tracks. One day she didn't come so I just went on without her. I was going to be late if I didn't. I started to crawl through the cars and somebody yelled, 'Hey Thelma, wait for me!' I turned around to look who it was and an engine hit that line of cars. It wasn't really a completely safe job.

"My aunt was taking care of my children. I had two then. The little boy got some aspirins and ate the whole bottle. We almost lost him. I thought, *Little lady, you'd better be staying home and taking care of your babies.* And that's when I quit.

"What I liked best about working out there in the yard was the idea, the knowing, that I was being patriotic. I wanted to do something and how do you know what to do? My husband came home one day and said, 'They're really hurting for laborers over at the repair track. I think you could do that.' I went over and, man, immediately they hired me! My aunt was tickled to death to keep my children.

"We cleaned the cars. One time they said, 'There's a boxcar out here with lampblack in it. We want that clean enough to put sugar in.' Boy, us girls really worked hard that day! Oh, it was so clean and nice when we got done with it. They really were going to put sugar in it—I suppose now you won't eat any more sugar.

"Quite often we went in the locker rooms and washed the lockers and cleaned all the tables. We'd sometimes bring some tuna cans from home and let the fellas put their cigarette butts in them so we wouldn't have to pick them up off the floor.

"I think they paid us about $1.35 an hour, something like that, but I didn't care how much it was—I was helping out, you know. And we really appreciated it. We really liked working there.

"We wore red bandana handkerchiefs and just old blue work shirts and bib overalls and men's work shoes. They were required, you know, because we could drop that metal on our feet and really hurt them. The bandanas were like the ones the railroaders wore around

Marjorie Taylor, Thelma Wilson, Dorothy Davis all worked during the 1940s. Photo taken in 2011 (photo courtesy of Christy Callendar)

their necks. We tied them up on top to make it look a little better.

"We did get awful dirty. The first thing we'd do when we got home was strip off and take a bath. We didn't just hurry. We appreciated having a nice hot tub to take a bath in.

"The men were very respectful of the ladies. Of course, my husband was right there to look after me. He worked in the car department too. One time I was cleaning the locker room. My husband was in there. I glanced around and he took a chew of tobacco! I didn't even know he chewed tobacco. He used to tell me, 'Go over to the store and get me a plug of tobacco to take over to Dick Pittman because he chews tobacco and his wife won't buy it for him.' There I was buying it for him all the time and didn't know it!

"I didn't work in the Canteen. My mother did. She loved working down there. The atmosphere was nice. It always surprised those soldiers when they came in and got all this food for free. The ladies felt like they were doing something to help their sons who were overseas.

"Once in a while when they'd have a wreck, the wrecker would come into the car department area to get fixed. They had a chef in the dining car. Us girls would volunteer to go in there and clean up their dining car for them. We'd clean the tables. We always got a little treat. They'd fix us some food and let us eat. We really liked that!

"We had this nice Mrs. Snyder that kept the locker rooms so clean. She kept a-saying, 'Don't put cigarettes in that toilet,' but one of the girls threw a cigarette in the toilet. Mrs. Snyder didn't know who did it so she shut off the steam heat in the locker room. We always put our lunch—you know like if we took soup—on that steam heater. We'd have nice hot soup at noon. Well, that day we had cold soup. The girls were a little unhappy with Mrs. Snyder.

"We didn't work at night, we just only worked in the day, seven until three. I know I got off early and got to take my bath and cook my husband his dinner before he got home.

"It's a wonderful place to work. They pay as well as anybody anywhere. There are a lot of rewards—like when you get old. Part of my retirement is from my husband's pension. I would be in a bad fix if I didn't have it. The only part I didn't like about it was getting so dirty. Otherwise I enjoyed it."

Frances M. Kemper Miller

Frances M. Kemper married Bernard Miller in 1917. They had eight children. At least three of the children were still at home when Frances began working for Union Pacific as an engine cleaner and laborer in the car department in the early 1940s. Marguerite Smith, the second oldest, is 90 now and lives in Maxwell. "It was money coming in. Those times were hard for everybody."

Marguerite's son Robert and his wife Linda were amazed by Frances. "She was busy all the time—a heck of a good cook too. She was a go-getter. We're not surprised she worked there. She ran circles around us and we were in our twenties."

Her son Marlin was five or six when his mother went to work. "She cleaned the pits out. She just got the wheelbarrow and hauled it out. She must of liked it because she worked there until she retired. It was kind of hard work for those old women."

Frances was born in 1900. She worked for Union Pacific for 21 years. She died in 1988 at age 87 and is buried in Floral Lawns Memorial Gardens at North Platte.

Frances Miller (1940s photo courtesy of Marjorie Taylor)

Lena Flock Edwards

Lena was a laborer in the car department who worked with Thelma Wilson in the car department in 1943.

Frances M. Bradley Walter

Frances M. Bradley was born in Elm Creek, Nebraska, July 9, 1910. She was a telephone operator when she married Thomas Walter in 1930. She hired out to work for Union Pacific during World War II as a laborer in the car department. She died in 1989 at age 79.

Clerks

Waneita Schomer

Waneita Schomer was born in 1923. She was 28 years old and making $140 a month when she dropped out of beauty school to work for Union Pacific as a clerk at a starting rate of $239 a month. When she began working, she and Margaret Durham handled the office together. Thirty-two years later when she retired, there were 25 in the office.

Waneita says:

"It was a great experience and of course I loved it. I loved every minute I worked for the railroad. In the old days we were in the old roundhouse where they had the turntables and all of that. We didn't have air-conditioning. We didn't have electric fans. No coffee pots. We girls went out and bought an electric fan for our office. We bought a coffee pot but we laughed about it. We didn't buy it for us because all the officials came in and used it. We furnished the coffee ourselves. It was quite different than it is now.

'When we worked in the old roundhouse, we had to wear dresses and in those days the dresses had to go to the dry-cleaners. We wore nylon socks and heels. You were dressed. Winter or summer we had to go in the yards with the payroll in dresses. When we moved to the diesel house we were allowed to wear slacks since the stairway we had to go up was open metal but until then we had to wear dresses.

"In those days clerks were paid a monthly salary so we did not get overtime. In 1971 when they were preparing to move to the diesel house, the younger set insisted that we get overtime and we did.

"When I was in the car department, I did everything. I was a secretary. I took dictation. I took care of the finances. The men made out time cards and I had to take certain things from the time cards and keep track of them

Frances Walter (1940s photo courtesy of Marjorie Taylor)

separately so they'd know where the money was going. I had to see that the mail got down to the last train. At the diesel house I did finance and I did some hiring. Of course I did training when the girl who worked with me moved to Omaha. When there was only two of us, there wasn't hardly anything that we didn't do. We worked supplies and at that time they didn't have computers. We had to write down a lot of things that today they don't. I retired the week they got computers in.

"I was there when they changed over from the old steamers to the diesel. It was quite a change because all the forms were different. They had no officer to do hiring then so I did it. I averaged 14 hour days for 14 months interviewing the many people who came in for jobs. The railroad bosses told me, 'You don't need to work like that.' I said, 'Come on, I'm not doing this for the railroad. The guys need jobs or they wouldn't be coming in.'

"I was born and raised on a farm so I was used to working with men and believe me, the men were very respectful. We didn't hear slang. We had no dirty stories. We had none of that. The men really respected us girls. They would help us and we would help them. It made life easier for everybody.

"I remember one time when one of the guys came in and I forget if it was the word 'darn' or 'damn' that

he used — not about me. The general foreman he was talking to took him aside. (I heard it all—their office was connected to mine.) He said, 'Don't you ever come in this office and use that kind of language. I don't care if we have a woman clerk or a man clerk, we don't allow that kind of language around this office.' In the 33 years

Shelley Meyer, unknown retiree, Janet Able, Betty Anne Parr, unknown retiree, Waneita Schomer, and Donna Fair at Waneita's retirement party (photo courtesy of Betty Anne Strawn)

I worked, we did not have any of that to put up with.

"Working for the railroad was great because you could get so much more wages than you could get downtown. There were women who kind of resented the fact that I got to work on the railroad. Not hate—but a jealousy on the part of the people who worked downtown because they knew that my pay was better. But they were very understanding. They knew I had a sick husband. My husband was sick in bed for six and a half years and the insurance only covered one year so I took in washings and ironings to make ends meet and I could stay home with him. The engine men, and others too, would throw in some money to help me out each month. They gave me about $70 a month. I have to admit that I still had a few bills after he passed away, but I got them all paid up in a short time. I was very grateful to the railroad, very grateful. And I'm going to say the people I worked with were very, very nice.

"I was employed 32 1/2 years and I never missed a day of work. One day it was so bad that the boss came and got us in one of the jeeps they had. One time he wouldn't let us drive home. He took us home. They were just wonderful people to work with."

Pauline Hora Maxwell

"I started my employment with the Union Pacific Railroad at the roundhouse in 1952. I was 23 years of age. It was a fun place. It was family. We enjoyed what we were doing. We worked together.

"The pay scale for women was just the same as men. It was because of the unions that you got it. It wasn't the railroad handing it to you. I belonged to the Brotherhood of Railway Clerks. We got the same pay as the men did but you were expected to do the same work. There were no exceptions to that. You did the same work. In those days women weren't expected to earn the same pay as men. Downtown I was a steno for attorneys and for the county attorney. I was making $135 a month. I started with the railroad and it was $298. I can still see that $298. I couldn't believe it. $298 a month. That amazed me.

"My job was doing all the typing and keeping track of things, doing the inspection forms and delivering mail.

"The typewriters were manual. My typewriter had a wide carriage because some reports had to be typed on wide paper. All reports were at least 10 copies and we used carbon paper. One report I remember was all the measurements of the wheels of each locomotive.

"Each foreman got a copy of letters, information and instructions. These had to be typed with carbon paper. Sometimes we had to type them twice to make the last few copies legible.

"Each employee had a timecard with their name and assignment to a certain foreman. These had to be sorted manually so each foreman, each shift, had their correct employee. When the timecards were turned in, the information on them had to be computed as to the work they did and a report of the total expenses. That report was called to the superintendent of the mechanical department in Council Bluffs. We would make sure we had all our questions and reports so that only one call was made.

"I remember when we got our first copier. It had a big cylinder and it had a handle that turned the cylinder. You typed a master sheet and the type perforated it so when you tore it apart all you had was the perforated sheet with the letters. You hooked it on to the cylinder. There was a solution in there. You wanted to make sure you didn't get too much solution or it would ruin it. You had to do it just right. When you turned the handle, the solution printed the letters through the perforations. You had to hand-feed the paper and hope that the master sheet lasted for as many copies needed. If not, you had to retype the master sheet.

"When the district foreman called for an investigation of an employee who possibly violated a rule or was lax in work and attendance, one steno-clerk had to

Pauline Maxwell (photo courtesy of Morgan Greenwood)

be there with the unions, foreman and witnesses. All conversation had to be taken in shorthand. All shorthand had to be translated and typed for all to read and sign. One investigation we had was so long it took two steno-clerks to compile all the records.

"All letters from the district foreman were dictated to the steno-clerk who typed the information for him to read and sign.

"The foremen's mail had to be delivered to them in the roundhouse and the back shop, and all timecards picked up.

"It wasn't the most exciting job, but I enjoyed what I did. I enjoyed working with the men.

"We wore dresses and nylons—in my job at least. The women who worked out in the yards and round-house wore coveralls. They were women who were hired during WWII. We had a lady by the name of Dollie McIntyre who was a turntable operator. She did her job tremendously well. The women engine cleaners were re-ally nice—and funny. They were competent and did their jobs well. They never complained. They were just glad to be working. When the men came back from WWII some of them went back home, but some of them stayed and were able to retire from that job. I enjoyed them and they worked hard. To me, the real and true heroes were these women who worked in the 40s and 50s and did the same work as the men. I never did hear any of them complain about their jobs or the dirt and grease. They were the pioneers for women so that women could work in all the crafts.

"The classifications for fireman/oilers were many: lye vat attendant, engine cleaner, hostler attendant, fire knocker, turntable operator, stationary engineer, sup-plyman, and laborers. Some women worked these jobs.

"The fireknockers opened up the ash pans and knocked the live fires out of the steam locomotives before they crossed the pits. They dumped the coals so the locomotive would just have enough steam to get across the turntable and into a stall in the roundhouse. They wanted it shut down then. Women operated the turntable which was a big responsibility. When the loco-motive got into the roundhouse, the fireman/oiler would put chains down in front of the wheels so the locomotive could not move.

"They did have some that went through the walls at the roundhouse. One morning I got to work and here's this big steam locomotive not too far from our office. It was something to see this big black locomotive sitting up there. It broke the chains or somebody didn't put

the chains down or something. And it happened before. It wasn't just a case of one time. The roundhouse had a brick wall. It didn't take them long to put it back up. Nothing was insulated like a house or like the diesel shop now.

"Sometimes the locomotive didn't get spotted underneath the exhaust stack. The roundhouse and back shop would be filled with smoke. You had cinders and you had smoke and ashes coming into the office on your clothes and hair. Those were the good old days. When it was really thick, the back shop would be so full of smoke that the pigeons that were roosted up inside of the building would drop to the floor dead. That was how bad it was.

"They had big pits in the back shop to run the diesel locomotives over. They had a big lye vat. The lye vat attendant could put parts in there and they'd come out clean of the rust or the paint or whatever they were trying to clean off. Very dangerous. The railroad had a machine shop, a tool and dye. The machinists could make anything that a steam locomotive needed. The back shop had a 20-ton overhead crane which moved parts from one end to the other.

"Boilermakers had to mix asbestos in a vat with a big board. They put this asbestos on the boiler of the steam locomotive with their hands and patted it down. This kept the heat in the boiler when the fire was built up by the fireman.

"The Union Pacific experimented with a pow-dered-coal burning turbine. It did not burn any oil. It made trips between Omaha and North Platte, but always had back-up power with it. I believe the 80-80B was just that, an experiment.

"In the 50s some of the passenger trains still had the steam locomotives. They were capable of 90 mph. Then the diesel units were put on passenger trains, but the railroad still maintained one steam locomotive to protect the passenger trains which came into North Platte early. This unit was the 844. It was taken to the depot every night and if not needed was put back into the roundhouse. The 800's oil burners steam locomotives were high powered and were designed for passenger trains. If late for arrival at a terminal, it could run 100 mph. Sometime in the 50s this 844 made its last trip to Cheyenne. Most all steam locomotives were dismantled but the railroad kept the 844.

"I worked in the car department for a while. It was west of the roundhouse. In the 40s there were three women that worked with the men carrying brake shoes to the carmen and other jobs.

"I worked in the roundhouse as an engine dispatcher midnight to eight for years calling engineers and firemen. I enjoyed that very much. The office of the engine dispatcher, like the rest of the roundhouse, had a certain amount of small critters such as rodents, cockroaches, and other insects. The engine dispatcher always had something handy to hit the critter.

"The engine dispatcher had a blackboard that covered one wall with all the names of the engineers and firemen, switch engine crews, passenger train crews and the time they were called. Chalk was used to record all this. You stood on a long ladder to write the time and the locomotive numbers next to the names of the crews. When it rained, you almost had to have an umbrella to make sure the rain did not wash the chalk off the blackboard.

"At the diesel shop I did all the assignments, did the bulletins, and did the paperwork when we hired people. Then we had that big, big layoff in the 1980s. I think we laid off a hundred people out of the diesel shop that year. It was the saddest time of my life. They abolished all these jobs. People had to move. They had to sell their houses. They all had to go find work somewhere. It was a tough time. Back then you didn't draw much unemployment. You can't support a family on that. As they needed more help we could call some of these people back, but some of them just left the country. It was devastating. It was a big loss to the railroad too to have all this training leave town like that. I hope it never happens again.

"I worked there 30 some years. I have been retired for 23 years and have always been glad to have had the chance to work for the Union Pacific Railroad."

LeNore Elizabeth Fletcher Weekly Gale

LeNore Gale was born in 1916 and died in 2000 at the age of 84. She was hired as a clerk during WWII and worked for nine years. Her daughter Julie Seip says, "My mother liked the work. It was challenging and she probably would have kept working but she wanted to stay home with me and my brother."

Waneita Schomer took LeNore's position in the diesel house in 1953.

Margaret Durham

Margaret Durham worked as a clerk in the diesel shop with Waneita Schomer. Pauline Maxwell remembers

her fondly, "She was very accurate and personable. She had a beautiful laugh and a beautiful face."

Alice Fitzpatrick Blalock Thalken

Alice was born in 1892. She graduated from NPHS in 1910 and attended Kearney Normal School. She taught in rural schools in the North Platte area. In 1917 she married Harold Blalock who died in 1944. She married George Thalken in 1947.

During WWII she worked in the yard office in North Platte and was active in the Red Cross.

She died at age 94 and is buried in the North Platte Cemetery.

Helene M. Rehn Rutt

Helen Rehn was born in 1911. She married Victor Rutt, a high school teacher. For 33 years (from 1943 to 1976) she worked as a clerk for Union Pacific, retiring in 1977. She died in 1992 at age 81.

Pacific Fruit Express (PFE)

Pennie Mattke

"I was a clerk at Pacific Fruit Express from 1952 to 1954. I saw the opening listed at the employment office. I applied because I wanted something different—and it really was. At first I worked in the PFE offices and then I moved to where the UP clerks had their offices. PFE had just one little corner there with two desks.

Two different times I went to Omaha to help with filing in the UP offices.

"I walked from 820 E 5th to Oak Street, rain or storm, and rode the rest of the way with a woman I worked with. We went to work at 4:00 P.M. and got off at 11:00. I don't remember now what I did exactly. That was a long time ago. I know I helped keep track of cars and break trains apart. Once in a while we had a lost car and I helped find it. The papers we had for the cars were held together with ordinary straight pins rather than paper clips and sometimes I pinned them wrong because I do some things left-handed. It's funny the little things you remember. Mostly I did what they asked me to do and they paid me.

"I got married in 1955 instead of going to Kansas City to continue with PFE. My husband and I raised five children."

Management

Jane L. Drummy

Jane was born in 1920. She graduated from Omaha Technical High School in 1938 and married Samuel Drummy in 1942. They moved to North Platte in 1947.

Jane was employed by Union Pacific for many years. She was the administrative assistant to the assistant superintendent when she retired in 1983.

Her daughter Tad Lisella writes about her mom:

"The UP was a huge part of our lives in North Platte. My mom worked in the roadmaster's and train-master's office over the years in spite of having seven children at home. She had wonderful friends there... probably kept her sane!

"Over the years I've run into people who knew Mom and worked with her. They frequently comment about what a wonderful, helpful person she was.

"When the depot was demolished, it meant a change in Mom's work situation. She was accustomed to working as the only clerk in the office. When those offices were moved out to the yard she knew she would be working with several other women. The thought of this change was a little frightening for Mom, but she ended up enjoying her new work situation and made some lifelong friends."

Jane died in 2001. She was 80 years old.

Irene Cummings Gorman

Irene was born in 1920. She worked for Union Pacific for 38 years. After she retired, she moved to Lincoln, Nebraska.

Tom Gorman writes:

"Irene Gorman was my aunt. She was married to Lynn Gorman who owned O'Connor Drug Store. I think that Lynn was about 60 years old when he married Irene. He and Irene had a great time going to Nebraska football games. I have been told that Irene was like the 'manager' of the UPRR in North Platte as she worked with the top people of the railroad for many years."

Janice Martin writes:

"Irene was hired in the day that people were given jobs according to their ability and work ethic. She was able to obtain a high supervisory position because she knew how to run the office. She was a capable admin-istrative-type manager. She was trusted and given lots of responsibility by her boss Bud Guynan. She was all business."

Jane Drummy (photo courtesy of her daughter Tad Lisella)

DeLoyt Young writes:

"When I was a special agent and a yardmaster I enjoyed working with Irene very much. She was a dear friend as well. She was very knowledgeable and a good railroader. She was there over 30 years and was at the point that what Irene said, went. She basically ran the railroad."

Engine 3932 (1940s photo courtesy of Marjorie Taylor)

Timeline

1866   Union Pacific track completed to North Platte

1868   Roundhouse and turntable built in North Platte

1869   Union Pacific Depot and Hotel built

1881   Roundhouse blows down

1895   First telephone in North Platte

1897   E.H. Harriman purchases Union Pacific at an auction in Omaha

1902   Year-long strike by machine shop workers begins

1907   Minnie McCoy, first documented female Union Pacific employee in North Platte, is hired

1910   North Platte gets double track

1913   New 28-stall roundhouse built

1915   The Union Pacific Hotel and Depot burns

1917   The Union Pacific Depot is rebuilt

1919   Nebraska gives women the right to vote

1941   The North Platte Canteen begins

1946   End of the North Platte Canteen

1948   The west retarder yard (42-track hump yard and Union Pacific's first automatic classification yard) replaces 20-track flat yard

1957   Florence Stamp is first woman to retire from Union Pacific in North Platte

1963   Congress passes the Equal Pay Act as an amendment to the Fair Labor Standards Act prohibiting pay discrimination based on sex

1964   Title VII of the Civil Rights Act makes it illegal to retaliate against a person because of complaints about discrimination

1967   President Johnson's Executive Order 11246 enforces affirmative action

1968   Double-hump, 64-track classification yard for eastbound traffic opens and is named Bailey Yard for Union Pacific President Edd Bailey who was born in North Platte

1969   Philadelphia Order by President Nixon guarantees fair hiring practices

1970   Eastbound hump yard constructed

1971   Roundhouse and machine shops razed
Streamliner passenger service ends
New diesel repair shop opens

1972   Title IX of the Education Amendments prohibits exclusion from participation in any education program on the basis of sex
The Equal Employment Opportunities Act establishes outline of regulatory reform in the railroad industry

1973   Opening of "one-spot" car repair facility
North Platte depot and icing platforms torn down

1976   Railroad Revitalization and Regulatory Reform Act prohibits discrimination on the ground of race, color, national origin or sex and requires affirmative action to remove or overcome the effects of prior discriminatory practice or usage
Carol Townsend becomes first woman engineer for Union Pacific in Nebraska

1979   New communication and multi-purpose building opened at Bailey Yard

1980   New 50-track westbound hump yard opens.

1992   The westbound coal yard expanded and computer-aided dispatching installed

1994   Eastbound fuel facility opened

1995   New westbound fuel facility opened

1995   Bailey Yard was officially recognized in the Guinness Book of Records as the world's largest rail yard

1996   Union Pacific/Southern Pacific merger creates nation's largest rail system

2009   Lilly Ledbetter Fair Pay Act releases gender-unequal pay from statute of limitations

2011   History of the women of the Union Pacific, *Powering UP*, is published.

Section III

Women of
Affirmative Action
to 1990

Introduction

In the years following World War II, the percentage of employed women in the United States dropped. The same was true at Bailey Yard though more women continued than after World War I. In succeeding years, more women were hired. The transportation department remained a man's domain.

A new culture of domesticity (perhaps due to television programs like *Father Knows Best*) appeared across the country. Women married young and suburbia flourished.

Beneath this tranquil way of life flowed underground streams of discontent. College-educated mothers wanted more for their daughters. Discussions of civil rights, equality and justice gushed through college dorms. The Vietnam War flooded the country with revolutionary emotions. In 1961 President John F. Kennedy created the President's Commission on the Status of Women and appointed Eleanor Roosevelt to lead it.

Support for the family and motherhood was firm in the commission's 1963 report. The report also revealed that women were not paid equally with men and that discrimination existed in the workplace. The Equal Pay Act of 1963 used legislation to correct the inequality. The Equal Employment Opportunity Commission (EEOC) was created in the historic Civil Rights Act of 1964 and an amendment to it prohibited employers from discriminating on the basis of sex. In the late 1960s the second wave of feminism became part of the civil rights movement.

In 1967 President Johnson's Executive Order 11246 to enforce affirmative action was amended to cover discrimination on the basis of gender.

In 1969 the "Philadelphia Order" initiated by President Nixon guaranteed fair hiring practices in construction jobs and required federal contractors to show 'affirmative action' to meet the goals of increasing minority employment.

In 1972 the Equal Employment Opportunities Act established the basic outlines of regulatory reform in the railroad industry.

The Railroad Revitalization and Regulatory Reform Act of 1976 contains a section of nondiscrimination clauses. Not only can there be no discrimination on the ground of race, color, national origin or sex, but affirmative action must be taken to remove or overcome the effects of the prior discriminatory practice or usage.

Union Pacific complied quickly with the government regulations and in 1976 the first woman engineer, Carol Townsend, took the driver's seat in the cab of the train.

I may sometimes be willing to teach for nothing, but if paid at all, I shall never do a man's work for less than a man's pay.

– Clara Barton

Carmen

Bonny J. Mitchell Branting

"I come from a long line of railroaders. My grandfather Harry Mitchell was a steam locomotive engineer and a passenger service engineer. My dad William Mitchell (machinist), my stepfather Lyle Miller (diesel shop superintendent), my brother David Miller (engineer), my sister Shirley Tuenge (switchman) my brother-in-laws Victor Lockard (engineer) and Tim Coffman (conductor) and Michael Tuenge (engineer) all have over 30 years service. My husband Robert has been a carman for 28 years.

"I started my railroad career in 1976 in the transportation department as a waybill and data processing clerk. I was 21 years old. This was the period of time when tag (punch) cards made of thick paper were used and fed into a big printing machine. Computers as we know them now were not invented as yet.

"The cards were made of thick paper. A stack of cards was put into the IBM punch machine and clerks typed a card for every car. A hole was punched for every piece of information: car initial, car number, load or empty, contents of car, car origination, car destination and a shortened version of the destination, for example, SP5 was the tag meaning this car was going to be routed UP to the off line railroad of SP (Southern Pacific).

"North Platte is a classification yard. After each car was humped, it was put into a designated track for same destination cars. Information for each car was obtained off the waybill that followed each car from station to station along with a 'wheeler'—a list of cars on a train with the information above. The punch cards were inserted in the wheeler machine producing a nice printed list.

"As the trains arrived at North Platte, the conductors delivered the waybills and wheelers to the yard office clerks. The yard office clerks put each waybill into a 'pigeonhole' for each specific destination, such as, all Los Angeles traffic went into the same pigeonhole. There were about 30 pigeonholes at each desk. After 3- 5 trains arrived and all cars were humped, the same destinations were all put together and a new train was made. We called it blocking a train.

"If a waybill ended up in the wrong pigeonhole and the freight car was physically humped into the wrong track, it was known as a 'wahoo in the train'. This was not good as the freight car was headed for the wrong destination and on the wrong train. It was a good way to get in trouble.

"When the new train was all put together and the waybills with punch cards were in the same sequence as the train, the punch cards were pulled from the waybills and stacked and put in the wheeler machine. Then a wheeler was run and the waybills and wheeler were given to the conductor to take to the train and head out of town. Once the wheeler was run, the punch cards were secured with a rubber band. The cards were kept for several months in the storage room with a copy of the wheeler. Keep in mind this was before computers. When computers arrived on the scene, it was a whole different operation. All the information was transmitted through the computers to the next station and waybills were all electronic. Now, at any time, a customer can run a car inquiry and find out where their freight car is and when it will be delivered.

"I do have to tell you about my favorite job at the Union Pacific. Have you heard of station agents? I was 'fill-in' for the station agent when he went on vacation a couple of times. I would arrive at work, dispense the mail for the day for the entire Bailey Yard, then get into a Chevy Citation and head to Brule, Nebraska. I'd stop at all the grain co-ops on the way back to North Platte and visit with them about how many loads they wanted picked up or how many empty grain hoppers they wanted spotted so they could fill them with grain. The co-op might want 20 empty hoppers or 20 loaded hoppers picked up or put on a train. The 'local train' would then work at each co-op and spot or take cars and bring them to North Platte for classification. Each visit I was offered a cup of coffee and sometimes a doughnut! It was a fun job meeting the customers face to face and hopefully make them happy with our service of grain cars. In comparison, now the co-ops have access to the

UPRR website and can order their own cars 24/7 without waiting for the station agent to arrive. There is no longer a station agent in North Platte as the computer replaced him or her.

"As time went on, I also worked in the maintenance of way department as a clerk taking care of payroll and ordering material and supplies for construction of the new Bailey Classification Yard. After completion of the new yard, I worked for the diesel shop as a tower clerk recording locomotives that came into the diesel shop for repairs to be performed. After that I returned to the transportation department as a crew caller. That job consisted of calling engineers to work.

"In the early 80s I was a material scheduler for the diesel shop. Computer terminals were at most work sites. In 1984 customer service center was established at the yard office and in 1986 the customer service center was moved to St. Louis for centralization and to downsize the clerks. My only options to hold a job on the UPRR were to move to St. Louis or to go to a schooling in Omaha for six weeks. At the time I had two toddlers and a husband and found it a hardship to tear the family apart. The company offered a buyout which I accepted in September 1986.

"During the period of September 1986 through April 2005, I kept applying to get hired back on the railroad. I was told that I could not be rehired because I had taken a buyout. Finally my persistence paid off. I was hired on as a carman in 2005. At that time the company decided it was better to hire people with railroad knowledge and I was a good applicant. I served my time in the apprenticeship program and was a carded carman in April of 2008. I am one of twelve women in the car dept compared to 300 men.

"I am so very thankful for my job. I just can't imagine working anywhere else. The Union Pacific has taken good care of me and my family for many many years."

Clerks

Darlene Clemens Siegmann

For 27 years Darlene Siegmann was employed by Union Pacific Railroad in North Platte and her family is proud of her. Penny Adkisson says, "I was the only kid around with a grandma with a hardhat. I loved seeing her come off work in her skirt and heels and hardhat. Everybody loved her."

Darlene Siegmann, Donna Fair, Kristy Lage, Twila Brnyoff, Pauline Maxwell, Waneita Schomer (photo courtesy of Christy Callendar)

Darlene tells her story:

"Back in 1968 a good girlfriend of mine Gwen Pierson worked at the old roundhouse. She called me to say, 'You know they're going to be hiring when they get through with the new diesel shop. You'd better go put your application in.' So I did and I got hired as a crew caller and then as an engine dispatcher. As a crew caller I called the engine crews. The men used to go up to the old roundhouse and see how many times out they were and what was going on but when they moved out south on Front Street, the men would call to see where they were.

"When I was an engine dispatcher, the tower would call us to get the crew when they were ready to send a train out. We did the dispatching all by phone. We had the board with the names of the engineers and the firemen and the ones we called got moved to the bottom of the board.

"When they transferred all the crew dispatching and engine dispatching to Omaha. I went back to school to brush up on shorthand and then went to the car department as a steno clerk. If anyone needed help I could find the answer. Questions might involve safety glasses, insurance forms, safety shoes or W-2 forms. I also handled personal injury, leave of absence, and other reports. I paid bills and gave out checks. Now they mail checks. We used electric typewriters at first and when

electricity was off, we couldn't work. Then they got computers and we got used to them.

"When the diesel tower job opened up for days, I went back and worked up there. In the diesel tower I checked the list of units coming in to see if it was time for work on them. I sat up there a lot of years.

"I really enjoyed working for the railroad. At first when they hired us girls it was a little hard out there. Some of the older men, they didn't think we had any business being out there. 'This is a man's job. They should be called for this; they need the work.' And I'd say, 'They called me. They could have called a man.' Later on, guys treated us fine. Times had changed. It was great.

"The hard part was being familiar with all the rules. The fun part was when they'd bring in the new units like the 5000 and the 6900s. It was so neat to go out and see those and to learn about them.

"I worked all hours. My husband and I arranged it so one of us would always be home with the kids. Women had no problem working with the men. I'll never forget the one time I was about to get off work and one of the guys asked me to go out to eat. I said, 'Yeah, but just a minute. I'll go call my husband and he can get all four of the kids ready.' He never asked me again."

Darlene helped in the preparation of Union Pacific's television advertising program. As captain on the safety team Darlene traveled to see how other shops dealt with safety. She got a safety award for 13 years of service without a lost time injury. Today that safety still hangs in her head: "If I go into a store and see a rug twisted I have to flatten it down."

J. M. Santamaria, general director locomotive maintenance 1994 wrote a memo commending Darlene:

Dear Darlene:

I would like to take this opportunity to thank you for your consistent involvement in the safety of your co-workers and members of the local community. Your article on locomotive ditch lights along with your efforts on the S.W.A.T. Committee are right on target and underscore your commitment to safety.

Thanks again, it is involvement and commitment like yours that inspires others to become part of the team, and makes Union Pacific truly a safer place to work.

R. T. Bussard 1993 Director of Locomotive System Shop wrote:

It is employees such as yourself who continually strive to improve themselves, as well as their work environment that make the Union Pacific Railroad a world-class transportation company.

When the *Telegraph* got the following letter to the editor:

Letter: *A Toll on Families*

It was with a great deal of sadness that I noted the article in Sunday's paper regarding the Union Pacific Family Days Mr. Harlan Welton was quoted as saying, "It's a family-oriented railroad."

My thought is that the U.P. can keep their free yearly train rides, free hot dogs and their potato salad. This 'family-oriented" railroad can instead try to give back to my children the many months that my husband has been forced to be away from them over the past years.

If one dares to look at the divorce rate among U.P. employees it becomes apparent that the forced separations, due to jobs, take their toll on our families.

Sorry Mr. Welton, the 10,000 free hot dogs just don't quite cut the mustard.

Name withheld

Darlene had an answer:

I read "no name's" letter with a great deal of sadness. I wonder who forced her husband to work away from home. There are other jobs besides the railroad and he knew when he hired out his job would take him away from his family. No one forced him to stay in the same capacity. The Union Pacific encourages

its employees to attend college classes or other educational courses to further their careers.

I also noticed "no name" never once complained about the check her husband made. After working over 40 hours a week he makes more in one day than some men make working in five days.

"No name" evidently has not watched the expressions on the wide-eyed little ones as they climb aboard the passenger car for their first train ride or the smiles and memories brought back for the older ones.

"No name" has no idea how family oriented the Union Pacific Railroad really is. For example, a few months back one of our co-workers suffered a fatal heart attack while working on his roof. Immediately thereafter, a UPRR crew was dispatched to complete the roof.

When the tornados hit Grand Island, Union Pacific men and equipment were some of the first to reach the scene and during those horrible winter storms, how many times did the Union Pacific send out snowplows to help families in trouble? I could go on and on about the personal relationship between the Union Pacific and their families.

You mention the divorce among the UPRR employees. If a percentage was taken according to the number of employees and compare it with other businesses, you would not find it that high.

I can't help but wonder how many wives would gladly change places with "no name." At least her husband is working and for your information, quite well in this depressed economy.

Thanks to the 8,000 who did participate in making our fourth annual Family Days a success Hats off to the employees who donated their time and thanks again to the Union Pacific Railroad for making it all possible.

Darlene Siegmann

Joe McCartney, General Director of Public Relations and Advertising wrote:

Dear Ms. Siegmann:

Mr. Kenefick passed on to me a copy of your letter that appeared in the Telegraph. *We were unhappy about the earlier unsigned letter complaining about Family Days, particularly since it mentioned Harlow Welton who, as you know, is a tireless worker.*

We feel you did an excellent job of reminding everyone that Union Pacific is just what Mr. Welton and you have said, a railroad that cares about "Union Pacific people."

I thank you for coming to our defense and we will continue our traditions to keep you proud of being part of our family.

Summing up her years with Union Pacific, Darlene says:

"It was a good paying job and we made the most money probably of any of the women in town. I'd do it again. I'm proud of the good life I have now. I got a good retirement but I earned every penny of it. Working for the railroad made us a better life."

Joan Johansen

"I started working for the Union Pacific in October 1969. I was hired to fill vacations for the stenos in the office at the roundhouse about 18 weeks a year. The first day I worked, the job was abolished and I had a choice of working midnights as an engine dispatcher or quit. I had nothing to lose and everything to gain so I went to the midnight job.

"In those days, I had to 'break in' on the engine dispatcher job on my own time. Your pay started when you were assigned the job.

"I was a single mom with two children and had good grandparents to help me with babysitting. I was bumped about Christmastime because a clerk returned to North Platte from Cheyenne. Since I was the youngest in seniority, I went home for a short time. The clerk hired just ahead of me quit because of the uncertainty of steady work and I was therefore called back. When I returned, I worked a swing shift as an engine dispatcher or in the tower at the service track.

"The last ten years I worked in the diesel shop office. There I had an 8 A.M.- 4:30 P.M. job with Saturday and Sunday off—wonderful after the swing shift!

"In 1971 the railroad retirement board credited me with $12,207.47. In 1990 the amount credited was $34,073.36. I was always thankful that I had my job. The pay plus the benefits certainly gave my family and me a good standard of living.

"The people were interesting to work with. No matter what your question or problem, there was an 'expert' working somewhere in the shop that could help solve anything."

Bonnie North

"My husband left me in Nebraska when my son was 2 1/2 years old and my daughter was five days old and just one year after the death of my second child. He left me at my parents—gave me $20.00 and left. I knew I had to get a job right away to support my children. I went to work waiting tables at Merrick's when my daughter was just a couple of weeks old. I only had to

work there for about six weeks when my mother helped me get a job as a bookkeeper at St. Mary's Hospital. I worked there for about a year until I finally got on the railroad. They weren't fond of hiring single women with small children because they felt like you wouldn't be a good employee—that you'd miss a lot of work. I really had to prove myself. I was just thrilled to have a decent job and have insurance for my children and be able to take care of them the way I wanted to.

"I started as an engine dispatcher in August of 1971. I was laid off 61 times when I first started working. At one point I went to work at the Holiday Inn as a desk clerk and wondered if I would ever get back on the railroad. I had to move to Cheyenne to protect my seniority. I worked in Cheyenne for a year before I was able to come back to North Platte with a permanent position in the diesel shop. I worked in the diesel shop as a clerk for approximately 10 years. During this period of time I also worked in the car department. When my job was abolished at the diesel shop I worked as a bill clerk until all of those jobs were moved to St. Louis. I then worked in the superintendent's office until I was able to return to the car department, where I finished my career. I hung in there because of my children and the benefits that the railroad provides.

"When I first hired out most of the women were in the diesel shop. There were a couple that were engine dispatchers. It's definitely a man's world. We had to put up with a lot of discriminatory things. You got so you just let it go. You tried to overlook it as much as you could. It was really hard to advance unless you were willing to sacrifice a lot of your integrity. That's all I'm going to say on that subject.

"There were some people I thoroughly enjoyed working with. In the superintendent's office I worked for Tom Simon. I so admired him. He was a wonderful, wonderful man. I was able to use all my computer skills working as special projects clerk. You didn't get a lot of recognition for your hard work. I developed some health problems from working too much—a lot of weekends and nights but I survived. I made it through. I just kept telling myself that he pros outweighed the cons. I retired after 35 years. I was definitely ready. I was pretty burned out.

"My favorite job was in the car department. The employees were so easy to get along with. I had some really great bosses down there. You were kind of left alone to do your own thing, but at times it was very stressful. You worked with all different types of personalities, that's for sure. I dealt with over 300 employees, most of them men. There are some women now who are carmen. I was glad to see that they finally realized that women can do that job too. It took a long time for it to get that way.

"When I worked midnights I had to have two babysitters. I took my kids to the Baptist Church for daycare during the day. I'd get up and go pick them up, spend the evening with them, and then put them to bed. I had a sitter who came in and stayed with them all night. There were times when one of them was sick or something that I didn't get any sleep. It was very, very hard just having to prove myself, to prove that I was going to be a good employee.

"There were years when my kids were young that I had to work afternoons. That was hard. I missed a lot of time with them in the evenings. I don't think they remember that now. I think it was harder on me then it was on them.

"I remember holidays when I'd leave my mom with a whole kitchen full of dirty dishes and my children. My stepdad worked at the railroad too and we would go to work. It made me feel bad for her. My mom said, 'I'm glad you have a good job with the railroad but it irritates me sometimes. I feel like I've lost two of you to the railroad.'

"It consumes your life, especially those types of jobs like bill clerking and engine dispatching. Once you get established in an office job, you have weekends off. Then it's a lot different, but normally when your kids are little you aren't that fortunate to have an office job.

"One of my best experiences was when the 844 steam engine came through North Platte and I got to ride in it.

"It was all good. You have to ignore a lot of the things that go on around you. The language at times is pretty rough. You just have to learn to tune it out. You have people who yell at you. You can learn to yell back or just walk away. It takes a very strong woman to work out there. One of the gals I worked with had skin so thin that she cried a lot. I felt bad for her because she was a very nice person, but she just couldn't handle the stress and pressure of the job.

"We did have a dress code in the superintendent's office and in the diesel shop. We had to wear office attire. You couldn't wear jeans. In the car department they didn't care what you wore just as long as you came to work. Even the bosses in the car department wore jeans. It was a lot more relaxed atmosphere. I can honestly say that I really miss the interaction with everyone.

"There definitely are challenges and you have to be tough. I saw women come and go who just were not cut out to work out there. You have to have a strong personality with a strong desire to stick it out for the benefits to survive.

"I loved the car department. I loved the people there. I enjoyed the opportunities it gave me. I'm a computer person. In the superintendent's office I had a lot of wonderful opportunities to learn a lot about computers. In the car department it was the same way. Whatever I needed to make my job better, they gave me. So many wonderful people. I'd have to say that was probably my most enjoyable job.

"You know everybody thinks that women are gossips. Let me tell you something. They don't even compare to the men. Those men are terrible gossips. As a woman working in an office environment you don't even have time to think about gossip. Those are very, very busy jobs. Very busy.

"When I retired I was a senior mechanical administrator. I was like at the top of the food chain as far as clerks. At one time I thought about going into engine service or management, but when my opportunity came up to be an engineer, I just couldn't do it. My kids were little. I just couldn't see myself being gone. I know I gave up a lot of money, but I think my time with them was way more valuable than any money I could have made out on the road. I felt I was away from them enough the way it was.

"By the time I thought about a management position, I was older. It just wasn't worth it to me. I feel like I kept my integrity the years I was out there. I don't have anything to regret. I can't look back and say I wish I hadn't done that. The only thing I regret is the time I missed with my children—the holidays when they were younger and baseball games. But they survived and they're fine. It's definitely a sacrifice you make when you work out there. You don't have much of a life. You don't have time to even form friendships. You are so busy working that it just doesn't happen. In an office atmosphere there is no time to talk. You are busy all the time.

"My advice: Be prepared. Be prepared for the disappointments, the hardships. I know EEO exists out there but suing the railroad is not going to get you what you want. You're going to have to suck it up. Be willing to make the sacrifices you have to make to work out there. You can't take a lot of time off. You have to be totally committed to your job."

Judy Noonan

Judy Noonan

"I started out with the railroad in 1975 as an engine dispatcher, then I went to the diesel tower as a clerk. The object of that job was to assist the district foreman. I stayed there until I quit.

"I had worked for a county judge for 11 years. The pay wasn't really excellent. I loved the job, but the pay was so much better at the railroad, I went out and applied. The interviewer told me that I've have to start out just part time. I said, 'I can't work part time. I've got kids just starting college. I've got to work full time.' And so I left the interview. About three days later he called me and said, 'You know we never did discuss salary. I don't think you understand how much we pay out here.' I went back and he told me. I went to work for the railroad.

"I think the first week I worked about three days and the second week I worked about three days and that was the end of my part time.

"As an engine dispatcher I called crews to work and kept a lot of statistics—that about entails that job.

"In the diesel tower radios and telephones kept you in touch with the rest of the yard. First of all you started out talking with the chief dispatcher in Omaha—what trains you were going to run that shift or that day. You had to make sure you had an adequate number of locomotives to pull the train. They'd give you the size of the train and then you figured the horsepower that it took to pull it. We gave the orders to the foreman to tell him how many different sets of diesel engines were needed to pull what trains.

"We had a schedule. We had to keep in touch with incoming power and we had to keep in touch with outgoing power. We had to know what trains the east tower wanted to run and the westbounds. That tower dispatched everybody on the ground. You had about 60 on the ground and all around the yard. You were constantly on the phone and on the radio. It was very, very busy. But the time went fast. Of course there were days like any job that not much was happening. If there was a derailment somewhere, you're just sitting there waiting for tracks to clear.

"We liked to build ahead. We were keeping track of the units that were coming in. They had to be fueled and sanded. Any light repairs you couldn't handle at the service track, you'd send over to the shop.

"At first the chief dispatcher was here in North Platte. The engine dispatchers were moved to Omaha. They called them the engine dispatchers when actually they were crew dispatchers.

"I never had a bit of trouble. The men were always very gracious to me. When I started in the tower I was the only woman out on the service track. They could tell me anything. I didn't know the difference. But I didn't ever get upset with them. I had to kind of laugh with them. Like I'd ask, 'What can we do to fix this engine?' They'd say, 'Well, we're gonna change the sparkplugs.' There are no sparkplugs on a diesel engine. I thought that was hilarious.

"I will say I don't think I ever scraped frost off of my windshield. By the time I got down to my car the guys had scraped it off. They treated me awful good. I felt that we were all working together. It didn't make any difference if you were male or female.

"It was a good job. It's an excellent job for a woman in North Platte. The retirement's been fantastic. I was with them 23 years. I didn't retire. I quit. I had a close friend. Her husband was 63 or 64. He died of cancer. My husband was about 64 then and I thought, I wonder how long we've got together? My job didn't mean that we did or did not eat so I said, 'That's it. I quit.' It was the best decision I ever made. We've had 12 years together and fun.

"When I worked for the judge we had to dress to the nines every day to go to court. I didn't have the money but I had the clothes. When I started to work for the railroad, I could wear jeans every day. I finally could afford the clothes and didn't need them."

Betty Anne Parr enjoys her ride on the 8444 steam engine

Betty Anne Parr Strawn

"I was working social security. I was a single mom with three teenagers and I had to make more money. I thought, *Gosh, I'd love to work out at the railroad. I love trains.* I kept going out there, 'Do you have any openings? Do you have any openings?' I'd walk in and the guy would say, 'We don't have any openings.' After about three months I think he got sick of me. He said, 'We have an opening. Go over to the diesel shop.' And I got hired. And I loved it. I always worked the holidays because I needed the money and it was double-time.

"I started on the railroad in 1976. My first job was tower clerk, midnight to 8. The tower was located at the service track. You had 66 steps you had to climb. If the wind blew, the tower blew. If it rained, the floor was covered in water. I always thought I was going to get electrocuted, but I loved it. Located at the bottom of the 66 tower steps was the bathroom. In blizzards and rain you ran up and down those stairs. They did have a heater in the bathroom so it was warm.

"I loved going to work at the tower. You had to go across nine tracks. There were like 25 locomotives there. They'd all be running and the ground would be shaking. It was electrifying. I could hardly wait to get to work. When I'd get there, I'd say, 'Oh, I love the railroad!' I was one of those over-enthusiastic, positive people who nauseates some folks because I was so happy to be there. They were working midnights and they were tired.

"I worked with a district foreman up in the tower doing departures. You were responsible for recording the time it took the service track people to service a locomotive, who was involved, what time the engineer was called, the time the engineer arrived, the time the consist was ready and what time they departed.

"As tower clerk you typed the unit held report. You had to walk over to the diesel shop office around 3 A.M. to make copies for the foremen who arrived at 6 A.M. Sometimes the enormous diesel shop would appear like a ghost building. It could seem really creepy. Occasionally someone would whistle and when you looked around there wouldn't be anybody there.

"The district foreman knew I liked trains. When the 8444 steam engine came into town he said, 'Betty Anne, would you like to operate that?'

"I said 'YES!'

"'Get your hard hat on and your gloves. Somebody will meet you at the bottom of the stairs.'

"I got to back it up and drive it forward. The crew was on board. The fireman was there throwing coal into the firebox. I will never forget that as long as I live. That was just awesome.

"Eventually I ended up as an engine dispatcher. I did that about two years. We had two dispatchers—one worked the Cheyenne side and the other the Marysville side. We called the engineers to come to work. Sometimes you couldn't find them. You had the neighbor's number and where they liked to work out—you had all those numbers because you didn't want them to miss a call or they might get fired. Well, anyway, we thought they might get fired.

"I taught myself to be a stenographer and then I took a class at the community college. I took stenoscript. You can look at the word and almost tell what it is. I took shorthand too. I didn't like shorthand. Stenoscript was much easier.

"I got on days in the diesel shop office as a stenographer. This is where you took investigations, safety meetings and the meetings for the shop superintendent. I worked a lot of jobs there like time cards and all the paperwork for the new hires. I was there about four years. Nobody's perfect but I tried to be as perfect as I could when I took those investigations. I like pressure.

"I ended up at maintenance of way for a while. We had this enormous wall full of supplies. I had to speak a lot on the radio which kind of freaked me out. I was afraid I'd make a mistake and everybody on the railroad would hear me. We ordered supplies for all the people who were running around in maintenance of way. They'd call you and tell you what they needed. You got it ready and they'd sign off on it.

"I got bumped out of that job and ended up over at the car department. I was there about three months. I loved that job. I was the only clerk. That's when they started these safety exercises. Nobody wanted to lead so I did it. I was the only female over there. We'd form this huge circle and they'd all smile at me. I remember thinking, *How did I ever get into this?* They only lasted about 15 minutes. Pretty soon I could almost lead them in my sleep.

"My final job was midnights at the transportation department. I had a wall of videotapes. All the trains were taped coming in and leaving North Platte. If you had two or three trains coming in, you'd have to pull one video out and get the new one in quick. My eight hours went so fast—I was like a chicken with my head cut off. As soon as you'd get the tape out, you'd set it in a tray and a clerk would come get it. The clerk would go through the numbers on the cars and the locomotives, write them down and make sure that what was on the train was supposed to be on the train.

"There were many cubicles. I was on the other side of one when a girl inquired as to who she was working with that night. When she was told, 'Betty Anne,' she said, 'Oh no, she's so happy she nauseates me.'

"I worked ten years altogether and then I had to take a buy-off. I went to a year of community college and the railroad paid for that. They were really good to me. My daughter had heart surgery when she was in the eighth grade and they paid for that.

"When I was at the car department, they were doing commercials. I got picked to be in one. There were about 20 of us. We're all standing out there by the railroad tracks in our hard hats. We're singing, 'It's a great big rolling railroad...' So I'm in one of the commercials they have in Omaha.

"I'd tell a woman thinking about working for the railroad: 'Don't be afraid of mud or dirt or wearing a hard hat or your hair looking messy or working in the rain or in a blizzard. And don't be afraid if you have to use an outhouse because you're out in the middle of nowhere. You got to buck up. Be tough. No whiners. That's all. Just don't whine. You can do it. Anybody can do it.'"

Janice Martin

"When I was finally able to obtain employment with Union Pacific Railroad, I thought I had the world by the tail! I was to find out later that Union Pacific had me by the tail! My life had been fairly difficult financially prior to my hiring because I had three children to support. Obtaining a railroad job quadrupled my income. I wouldn't have to borrow $20 here and there from my parents for milk and bread until payday, and I wouldn't have to have food stamps anymore.

"National Secretaries Day was held annually with a huge party to celebrate the event. Each year the ladies from the railroad would come parading through the crowd of us other "peon" secretaries. They always looked so important and so impressive. I dreamed of becoming part of that entourage one day. The head lady's name was Irene Gorman. Irene was an astute-looking older woman. She had an air about her. How I envied those women to have such an important and good paying job. It became my goal to be one of them someday, somehow.

"As soon as I graduated business school in 1964, I applied at the railroad. As years went on, I kept being turned down with the excuse that they didn't have any openings. I decided to try one more thing. I wrote to the medical director's office in Omaha and asked why a "fat" clerk couldn't do the work. About a week later, here came a letter telling me that I was cleared for hire. I was elated. Two weeks later the railroad called and asked if I could be to work in one hour. I dropped everything and ran for the job. The date was August 14, 1978.

Janice Martin 1978

"A secretary named Jane Drummy needed some time off. They hired me until such time as she could return to work. She was very professional; her conduct, her dress, and her demeanor emanated that fact. Jane was kind and helpful to me. I had difficulty understanding the work. However, I was determined to get it.

"Jane came back in about 30 days. I found out that once the railroad hires you, you are expected to exercise your seniority wherever you can hold. I learned the job of morning report clerk to the dispatchers and placed myself on a midnight job. The office was filthy dirty. There were cigarette butts laying around everywhere; there were girly magazines in every desk drawer, small television sets to keep track of sports events; there was coffee slopped and spilled everywhere. Wastebaskets were running over with filth.

"A male employee looked at me and said, "This is a man's world. We don't want any women here. If you don't like it, you can quit and go home." I was afraid to say anything. Back in those days, EEO wasn't an issue. I was to learn later that I could have made a complaint and the company would have followed up even then.

"Working the graveyard shift was hard because I had a family to care for during the day.

"As time went on, the dispatchers got used to having a woman on the job. I asked to be promoted to train dispatcher, but at that time they didn't really want to promote women. You could have counted the number of female employees in North Platte on one hand.

"I moved from morning report clerk to the hotbox scanner detectors. What a boring job. I just had to walk around and around the room, pulling tapes that had readouts that gave a report on the condition of wheels from the trains that were out and running.

"The next job I had was what they called an 'N-O' operator. 'N-O' stood for North Platte Operator. The job required being able to take dictation from the train dispatchers giving out train orders and track warrants. Prior operators were required to send train orders via Morse code, but by the time I got to the railroad there were more advanced mechanisms to transmit these messages. The job required exact proficiency because the safety of train crews and equipment was involved.

"Working for the train dispatchers was challenging. It definitely taught me about the culture of the railroad. When all the train dispatchers were transferred to Omaha, it left a big hole in North Platte. Things just didn't seem the same. That was when I decided to bid over to the diesel shop area and see what life would be like on the mechanical side of the railroad.

"My job in the diesel tower entailed sitting five stories high in a small, square-shaped building with glass front and outside stairs they called catwalks. The toilet was down on the ground. The tower only held a foreman and the clerk. The inbound wash rack for locomotives was directly to the west of the tower. After the locomotives coming in from the road received their bath in the wash rack, they proceeded eastbound toward the tower where the clerk would write down all the numbers of the locomotives that were going on the pit. The employees working the pit would keep the tower informed of whether the locomotive was going to the shop for repairs or whether it was headed to the makeup track to go out on a train. The clerk made many reports and kept many records of the progressive care of the locomotives.

"A job opening in the diesel shop office came up that would mean working days with weekends off so I bid it. Every morning we had warm-up exercises. Then we would go to work on the stacks of locomotive reports and other things that we did. I did enjoy doing the newsletter for the shop.

"The large suburban vehicles that were used to transport crews to and from their trains were called paddy wagons. I was at the railroad for the money so I requested to be called for overtime driving paddy wagons. Through that experience I learned my way around the largest classification area in the world. I learned how the hump yards worked, the retarders, the fueling facility, the turnarounds, and the main lines. It was fantastic to see such a large operation work the way it does.

"After working a couple of years at the diesel shop, Donna Fair requested I bid over to the superintendent's office. Donna was well liked and had a great personality. I always wanted to work in the superintendent's office.

"Bonnie North and LouAnn Rochford were already working in that office. LouAnn was the receptionist. She did all the FRA reporting, among other things. Bonnie handled things having to do with the car department. My job was taking shorthand from the superintendent, making purchases of everything from pencils to railroad ties, and keeping track of the leased vehicles. I was also responsible for paying all the bills. I loved that job.

"When I first hired on I used a manual typewriter, then an electric one. Computers started to creep in about 1990. I kept hoping that they wouldn't make me use one, however one day I came to work and there sat the computer. My husband sat me down at home in the evening and explained how computers work. Each day at work I learned a little more and finally I was doing it—using a computer.

"One day my husband called to take me to lunch. He never took time off work to take me to lunch. I knew something was up. He had been asked to move to Omaha to take responsibility for an electronic repair shop. I loved my job in the superintendent's office. I loved my hometown of North Platte—but I left it all behind to begin a new life in Omaha.

"In Omaha I worked in the supply department, the mechanical department, the engineering department, human resources department and CMS (Crew Management System). In October 2008 I worked my last day and walked out of the door for the last time, retired after 30 years. I thank God that I had a good paying job all those years, with good benefits. I was able to raise my family respectably and without poverty. As I look back on the time I spent with Union Pacific, I have a lot of very good memories of the people I worked with and the enjoyable jobs that I had. I have to admit...I do love the railroad."

Twila Brynoff

"I hired out on the railroad as a clerk in the store department in 1979. I was 47 years old. Back then they had to have a woman to meet what the government said they needed to have in quotas. Helene Rutt retired and I took her place.

"The day that I was hired this young guy, young enough to be my son—probably young enough to be my grandson—got me on the lift truck. He says, 'Well, let's

just see what you can do. See those three fans piled up?' (They were huge ones like you put on a locomotive.) He says, 'Take that top one down, set it on the ground and back up. Get away from it a ways and then go back and pick it up and set it back up there.'

"The guys were probably standing around the corner thinking, *Hmm I wonder when she's gonna wreck that thing?* I suppose they thought they got a woman who didn't know sic'em, but I grew up on a farm with three brothers.

"At that time it wasn't cemented out there. The ground was rough. They didn't have the lift trucks with the forks that slide. I'd get them up in the air and about that time, the front wheel would go in a little bit of a hole and tip me to one side. I had to get around it and start it up again. Of course I wasn't afraid because I'd driven a tractor with a buck and stacker on it. I was used to things like that.

"After they started cutting jobs I wound up over at the yard office. I hauled crews. I did janitor work. I did everything there was to do. I worked in the office some and made waybills for the crews on the train. I used to clean cabooses too. That was a clerk's job, if you can imagine that.

"The caboose had a front door and a back door. The guys that broke me in said, 'This is how you clean 'em.' They'd open both doors and they'd do a little sweeping at one end and then they'd swoosh it out the other end. Of course they didn't sweep quite as good as I did. You put water in them too. On the outside there's a place to hook up a water hose. Turn the water on and it fills a compartment inside so they can flush their stools. If you didn't get it on just right, it would come off and spray you. It was a lot of fun.

"I was kind of known as the apple pie lady. I used to take apple pies to work. I'd tell the guys you bring the ice cream and I'll bring the pies. Of course the ice cream always showed up.

"When I first went out there I was wondering how it would be working around a bunch of men, but I could do as much as they did because I grew up on a farm and I was used to work. Had I known earlier what I know now, I think I would have hired out in transportation. When we first moved here though that was like, *A woman in transportation!* But that's where the big money was.

"At the time I worked for the railroad you had to wear a hard hat. You still do, but they were color-coded then. The store department's was yellow. The fireman/ oiler's was green. The electrician's was red. It was kind of neat you knew what craft. The machinist's was blue. Foremen wore a white cap.

"I can remember when our boss would say, 'We've got company coming today.' Company was always a big shot. 'Don't you guys go down around the coffee machine. I want you to get out and get lost like you're busy.' I could always find something to do. I could always go down and stock shelves or clean shelves. Stuff like that. I could always keep busy.

"They had what they called filter parties. That's before all this automation got in. They'd have these boxes, three or four feet square. We'd have to take them out of the trailer that brought them in and walk down the dock and put them in the storage trailer.

"At that time the railroad had a couple gas stations about ten miles out of town. Gas was piped into town. You had to make sure all the lines were open. We'd have tankers come in and we had to pump it out of the tanker into the storage tanks. I did that too. It was kind of challenging. Kind of different.

"I did everything out there. I can't say what I really liked best. I just liked being busy.

"The store department was the one that ordered all the materials for the railroad. You had to go out and count your nuts and your bolts, the washers and everything that they used—even the letterings that they put on the sides of the units when they painted them. Everything came through the store department. Sometimes it took quite a while to count them.

"I spent probably the first six years in the store department and after that I got bumped around. I'd help unload these piggybacks that'd come in on the trains. Like I said, I did everything.

"The kids were pretty well grown by the time I went to work. It's kind of funny because my husband is a pk (preacher's kid). At the time I got married and started having kids, they thought you ought to be pregnant and barefoot and in the kitchen—you've heard that old saying. My husband told me I couldn't work unless it corresponded to the kids' school hours. The first job I ever had was at what was then called the Ryan Motel at Ninth and Jeffers.

"I always wore jeans with a pocket on them so I could carry my keys.

"I would tell a woman today—if she wants to work and not just be a figurehead—that it's a good place. It's probably the best money she'll make in North Platte. You only have to work five years to be vested anymore. It's a darn good job.

"I was there until '92 and then it was either take the buyout or go to Kansas City. I took the buyout and spread it over two years. I wound up with 14 years service. Best job I ever had. Best pay I ever had. And I really loved the work."

Donna Jones

"I always wanted to work on the railroad. I rode the passenger trains when I was a kid. My great-great-grandparents way back to the beginning of time worked for the Union Pacific. My dad worked for communications and I played in the depots in Rawlins and Cheyenne. I'm what we call a foamer. It's in my blood.

"I hired out in 1980 in Hinkle Yard in Oregon as a clerk and telegrapher. I was a picl clerk (picl clerks pulled waybills), inbound and outbound clerk, biller and chief clerk. I sold Amtrak tickets and supplied the engines and the cabooses. I had a local there. I posted embargoes. I went to the shippers, picked up waybill information and typed stuff up. I gave roll-bys to the trains. It was a do-everything type of job.

"I closed the depot there in 1983. Then I worked with the MO_Pac merger. There were a lot of layoffs. I moved to La Grand, Oregon, where I was telegrapher and outbound driver. I shagged a lot. I went through alleyways and whatnot, dogs chasing me, to knock on doors to tell crews they were called.

"I put in a Rule 15 to come to North Platte. They had two zones for the clerical department at that time: the telegraphers and PBX wire chief operators were one department and all the rest of the jobs were the other. I was a qualified telegrapher. I also was qualified on just about every other job in the clerical so I worked the extra board and the furlough board. They put me whatever they needed me, but they didn't like crossing the zones. They kept putting me on temporaries. After your three-year probationary period, you had to work a job for thirty days to get your guarantee. They kept cutting me off on the twenty-ninth day. I finally said, 'You know, I'm qualified here.' I got my guarantee. That was good because a lot of people didn't.

"When I worked there they were phasing out the job of wire chief. I was the last one. I sat with the headset and plug just like a telephone operator.

"I worked waybills. Each car's waybill lists the shipper, the commodity, the weight, who it's going to, the origin and destination station, the route and any special instructions. The waybill had to ride with the train. We'd pull those, line them up in order, run a track list and work orders, bundle them and send them out with the orders the telegraphers issued.

"Back then we were still calling the crews. We had a tag system. Each crew member had their little tag and we had a Plexiglas window with cup hooks. Tags were moved up and down the hooks in the order that they were to be called next. If they did not have a telephone and lived within five miles of the origin of work, we would go to their home and give them their calls. It was kind of scary sometimes in the middle of the night. We eventually went to a written format. In the end it was all relocated to Omaha and put in computers.

"I learned to be a telegrapher just like everything else. You sat with somebody and just listened for a day or two, depending on how smart you were and how desperately they needed you. Then you would try it. But it had to be accurate. There couldn't be any errors.

"We still had the old manual typewriter that you had to slam the keys down on. Instead of typing, I would write the orders. My handwriting was horrible because I'd scribble as fast as I could to keep up. I'd go type while the others were doing their orders. I'd read it back to make sure it was accurate and sign it. I didn't have to send by Morse code. That stopped a few years before, thankfully.

"We used to have a card machine. We had twelve-by-four inch cards. Each card designated a railcar. You fed the cards through a machine and they shot out into stacks. Before that they did it by ticker tape—by teletype. They were holes in the ticker tape designating the orders. The holes were in Morse code.

"The tape got about four feet deep on the floor—just miles and miles of ticker tape. When it came out of the machine they read it and it would just go on the floor.

"The clerks were still doing telegrams then. They did them by telegraph before they switched to teletype. Then to the PBX and then the computer.

"I worked the scanner job that looks for hotbox detections. They had just gotten a new computer system in the dispatcher's office in Bailey Yards. It was a great big wall online that showed where the trains were. We watched that. If one of the journals looked hot we had to take it down to the corridor manager who would make the call to stop the train. They'd tell the crew to go out and walk it to see if it was on fire. You didn't want to miss one. It was pretty intense.

"I went to Saint Louis when we centralized everything at the National Customer Service Center. Five

thousand people did what two hundred fifty thousand clerks had done. You had to think what they had done physically and match that to what the computer wanted. The computer wouldn't let you unload that car until you'd done everything that had physically been done all the way up the line. There was no skipping steps. By that point we were pretty much cutting over into TCS (Total Train System), the system from the TIS.

"I worked three different computer systems, starting with the original one which was COIN—the IBM system. Then we had TIS—Union Pacific's internal system, and when we merged with MOP, it was the TCS that we are currently using.

"The computers have definitely done away with my craft. We did everything by hand. To clear orders, you got on line with a bunch of dispatchers, got the headset and stuck the plug in. We would get train orders over the headset which was connected to the PBX system. Everything was internal. We copied the order, repeated it back, date and time stamped it, rolled it up, and sent it out with the crews.

"It's tougher for a woman to climb up on a train. We don't have the same physical makeup as a guy. Guys are stronger in the upper body. You've got to find a way of compensating. We used to climb on and off moving equipment. Now they'll fire you for it. I always found it difficult because I'm a klutz. You have to get on and off with the right foot or you end up on your face, tumbling down the ballast.

"Working in a man's environment has been quite interesting. It has definitely evolved. You never showed that you were going to cry. If you showed any weakness, they would go straight for it. There were a lot of females I worked with that just did not make it. We had one gal who would cry every single day—but she came to work in a dress and spike high-heeled boots. Try climbing up and down on the trains like that. You can't do it. They would tease her and she would cry and cry.

"Working on call 24/7, 365 days a year —it's not a lifestyle for everybody.

"Currently I'm back to the first job I was doing. I'm a driver. It was pretty easy to come back to North Platte into everything that I've been doing for years. I like to haul the crews. I like the atmosphere in the transportation department. I still get to see the trains. I get to sit between them. I can feel the rumble and hear the bells and whistles. So here I am—right where I like to be, driving around, hopefully getting us all where we're going safe and sound, smiling and laughing."

Gwen Rae Foust Pierson

Gwen was born in 1939. She went to work in 1969 as a clerk in the diesel tower. When she retired she was a yard office supervisor. Gwen was active in union affairs and the Union Pacific Employees Club.

She died in 2009 at age 69.

Pacific Fruit Express (PFE)

Anne Miller

"When I came home from my second year of college in 1978, I was looking for a job. I hired on with the Union Pacific. I liked it and I stayed until I took a buyout in 1997. I was a clerk with Pacific Freight Express. I worked in the main office as timekeeper and did labels and insurance.

"UPFE used to water the hog cars that came through NOP. I did that too when I first started. It was a dirty, stinky job during the heat of the summer.

"In the winter we would work loads that had heaters installed in one end of the car. These heaters were probably three feet tall. We'd have to secure them in the cars and light them. It was very difficult in the old yards. We had to carry two heaters across trains to get to the track our car would be on. Once the new yards were built you could drive between tracks. I'm guessing, but I'd say each heater weighed at least 40 or 50 pounds.

"All kinds of loads came through the yard. We had cars of fresh produce, fruits, meat, roses, Christmas trees and lots more. We had to pull the waybill for every car and check the refrigerator cars. In North Platte, UPFE had a couple of tracks specifically where the refrigerator cars would be cleaned out by laborers. Carmen would service the refrigerator units and the diesel engines that provided power to run the units, and clerks would fuel the cars.

"The waybill would tell who the shipper was, the origin of the load, where it was going, its total weight, and the temperature to maintain. We'd read the temperature and fuel gauges on the cars. If the temps weren't within range, the carmen would fix the unit.

"We took care of diverts—cars we pulled to the side that didn't meet inspection. Sometimes cars would need to be diverted to another origin while in route because of a change in market needs. Union Pacific was very accommodating when that happened. Sometimes if there was spoiling freight on board, it was sold locally. A lot of the fruit trains or perishable trains coming out of, say California, would be totally perishable cars. You could often tell by the train name where it was coming from and going to.

"When I was ending my railroad career there were new prototypes of cryogenic cars. Those are cars that are cooled by a gas blown into them.

"In the 70s women were a minority for sure and you had to prove yourself to be accepted. The highest number of employees that we had while I was working was 223 and probably only six were women.

"I sure enjoyed my time on the railroad.

"I currently live in Pocatello where I went back to school and got my masters degree. I'm a LMSW, licensed master of social work. I work for the state of Idaho with Adult Mental Health as a clinician doing mental health assessments, individual and group therapy. I am a Designated Examiner (D.E.) for the state. As a D.E., I am involved in determining if a person because of a mental illness is a danger to themselves, others, or gravely disabled."

Crafts

Kristy Baade Lage

"I hired on in 1980. I resigned in 1993 because I got married and moved to Arthur. My husband didn't want me traveling back and forth.

"I started as a fireman/oiler. Within a few months they gave me an electrician apprenticeship. I got laid off from that and went back to work as a fireman/oiler. I was laid off again so one summer I worked maintenance away on a track gang at Hastings on a grain siding. They brought a bunk car for me to live in. Next we went out to Kansas and worked on a bridge siding. It was really hard work.

"The first day there were eight of us. We unloaded twelve hundred ties. My arms were burnt and just covered with creosol. By the end of the summer, it only took me seven swings to drive a spike. My hands were just numb in the night. I would wake up from the vibration of driving those spikes. I ran a jackhammer and everything. It was really physical work. I wouldn't have been able to continue so it was a good thing it was just a short-lived summer.

"I also worked in Denver under the 23rd Street Bridge where Coors Field is now. We serviced and fueled locomotives. It was a great experience. It kept my benefits going. Otherwise I would have been laid off and not been paying in to railroad retirement to keep my health insurance benefits all intact. It was sort of scary

Kristy Lage on Desert Storm engine

because there were guys there that had escaped from the mental hospital. They would be sitting up there on the locomotives in white gowns. The guys I worked with were all real protective of me.

"That fireman/oiler job—now that was something where you did everything from scooping out pits, to driving a truck, to driving a forklift, to sanding the locomotives, to fueling them, to cleaning the potties. That part was awful. You had a bucket and you had to go there and dump the... you know. That was before they put in the ones with the chemicals that had a big hose and you didn't even have to mess with it. When I first hired on it wasn't a very sanitary job—sort of like being a nurse with the bedpan.

"We washed locomotives and scrubbed them with big brushes. We cleaned the locomotive cabs out because the guys would just trash them—newspapers, sunflower seeds, pop cans, coffee cups, old sandwiches...

""Eventually I got back to my apprenticeship. It was a three-year apprenticeship. I always worked beside a carded electrician. We also went to the Voc Tech and had classes. There were some really great guys out there like George Shaefer and Cecil Burnside—some really great electricians. I had some great foremen too like Charlie Jones and Johnny Triplett.

As far as the apprenticeship, you did everything. We changed out whole generators, put in new fuel pumps, worked underneath changing out the traction motors and dropping the whole wheel out to unhook and cable them.

"I was a federal inspector on the service pit. I'd go through and make sure all the dates were on everything, all the light bulbs were in place, and all the stair lights were in. It was a good time for that apprenticeship because that's when all the locomotives went over from relays and contactors to computerized panels. We had to install a lot of new computer systems when they did modifications so the old locomotives would work with the new computer systems. It was a good learning experience. I enjoyed that.

"My grandfather was a machinist. When I was a little girl I went to the roundhouse with him. I always admired him and his buddies Pete Collins and Jack Schaffer. My grandfather retired, but they worked out there when I did so I always had those older gentlemen that were friends of my grandfather to look after me.

"When I graduated from high school I moved to San Diego for about a year and a half. When I came back at Christmas, my twin sister had hired on as a clerk so I put in an application. Then I moved to Boulder and made computerized circuit boards. I'd been working for about a year when UP called me for an interview.

"It was a big increase in the amount of money I was making and it was a good salary for a woman. There were some men that weren't appreciative of me being out there. They said I was taking a man's job who had a family to feed and that I shouldn't be there, that I should be downtown working in a bank or something because a man with a family needed that job.

"There was some harassment and stuff when I first hired on. There were these two guys who were sort of sketchy. They would pick on me when I was sweeping the ramps. They threw a broom down one time and said, 'Why don't you get on this and just fly this outta here?' I went to the foreman and told him about it. They sort of got in trouble. Well then they cornered me and said, 'You better just watch it. Some night when you're coming to work we're gonna be waiting in the parking lot and we're gonna blow your head off with a machine gun.'

"I was young. I just sort of took it. I think that if somebody out there said that to a woman in this day and age they would probably be dismissed. Some of the harassment that went on, you didn't want to go talk about or tell because then it got worse, the retaliation and stuff. A lot of it I just put up with rather than trying to make a wave about it. You know, the guys that were my age were good. And the older guys were all good. It was the guys that were about ten or fifteen years older than me that seemed like the ones that were just always wanting to...I don't know

"You could wear jeans, but I always wore overalls. I was pregnant out there with my oldest son. He's twenty-two now. The last couple of months they had me be on light duty so I could keep working. I wore big overalls and unbuttoned them so I could be pregnant in them.

"I've been away from there since 1993, I still have dreams like I have to get to work, or I'm at work.

"We had our cattlewomen region meeting with cattlewomen from other states. We took them on a tour of the diesel shop. When I walked in there, the diesel smell—to this day, I just can't stand it.

"I remember one time when I worked out at the service track it was like 70 below wind chill. It was freezing. Everything was freezing up, the air hoses, the fuel—it just about shut everything down during those big blizzards but they always seemed to keep things going.

"The railroad painted this locomotive like camouflage, the sand colors, in tribute to all the military going over during Desert Storm. We had to service it down at the depot. I have a picture of myself on that locomotive.

I worked there long enough that I will get a retirement. When I quit I was an electrician, and I was working as a relief foreman. Rudy Bussard was the shop superintendent. He was disappointed that I was quitting because I'd gotten that electrician's card. They were needing women for the numbers, I think.

"It was a good experience. I'm glad that I did it. I'm thankful that I had the opportunity. I got to buy a couple houses. It was good money for a gal."

Transportation

Carol S. Townsend - First Qualified UPRR Woman Engineer in Nebraska

"I started in the diesel shop in 1974 as a clerk. I worked a variety of clerk jobs, including the diesel shop, car department, diesel tower and engine dispatcher.

"The diesel tower was a control tower on stilts directing incoming and outgoing diesel locomotives, a small windowed office with room for two. We located and sorted out the diesels scheduled for inspections. One task was walking the packets of information to and from the nearby diesel shop. There was a hardhat rule that I just hated to obey. Walking back to the tower, I spot-ted two managers. Because I was minus my hard hat, I ducked around the corner to avoid being seen. I bonked my head on two hanging Safety First signs. I received a safety lecture I deserved that day.

"When I worked as an engine dispatcher, we had a unique system that kept track of the trains and crews. A large wall-mounted rack held nearly two hundred wooden blocks, each the size of a deck of cards. One's name was on each end—red for extra board, black for regular jobs. An extra board crewman, for example, would see his block on the bottom of the board. We moved the block up a notch for each train called. If you were five times out, you would get the fifth train.

"I was working as an engine dispatcher in 1976 when I heard they had to hire a woman as an engineer. That's when the government was insisting that the railroad hire women in previously dominated male positions. I was thinking, *Boy, those paychecks look good—maybe I should give it a try.*

"There was a lot of resistance. Some of the fellows knew that there was going to be a woman. The word was out. But they didn't know that I knew that it was going to be me. They'd come into the dispatcher's office, 'Well, I'm not gonna help her,' they'd say. 'This is not gonna work.' 'We don't want women out here.' When they found out it was me they said, 'Well, if we'd have known it was you, Carol...' You know, trying to backtrack.

"I spent a year riding trains—every day, six days a week—just getting ready to go to school in Cheyenne. In Cheyenne we had mechanical/electrical, rules, air, and hazardous material exams. It was hard for a woman. I had to almost memorize the material. To apply it—that was another story.

"After I came out of school they assigned me to an engineer for several months before they'd qualify me. Finally they rode with me and signed off. The next thing I knew I was marked up on the extra board. Now I was a block of wood in that big window with all those other blocks of wood. When you walked in, you checked the federal register, looked for your bulletins, and looked at your block of wood. Beside that would be the train symbol, date, and list of your power.

"When I got my first train I was scared to death. I just prayed I got a conductor who knew what he was doing and could help me, but we made it all right from point A to point B without any trouble. Every trip that I made, every train was different. Every set of power was different. I never worked with the same train crew more than once or twice a year because they'd rotate in

Carol Townsend – First Woman Engineer in Nebraska

separate pools. You're pretty much on your own. They finally got so they would accept me but I had to prove that I could do the job.

"I was so new that there were a lot of places we went that there weren't even facilities for women. No restrooms. Nothing for us. We just had to trail along behind the guys and do the best we could.

"The first time in Council Bluffs, I was tagging along behind the crewmen and followed them through the open doors of the men's room trying to keep my eyes straight ahead since I was surrounded by the tall china. Next trip I found a small separate ladies room, but it had been turned into locked storage. It took some convincing to get an extra key just for me.

"A student trip to Marysville was a nerve shaking experience. Near Edgar our coal train collided with a semi-truck and flatbed trailer carrying a tractor and combine. Our crew dived to the floor for protection and held onto the equipment racks, bracing for impact. The collision forced the trailer under the nose of the locomotive, derailing us. A train loaded with 15,000 tons or more of coal does not stop quickly. I was having quite a time staying on the floor riding that bucking bronco, holding onto the chair post with all my strength. Fortunately the brakeman was able to wedge his body against mine, keeping me in place.

"I can still vividly recall the sounds of the twisting and tearing steel and remember the impact as each car piled upon the other, ramming our set of derailed locomotives and spilling their loads one by one, seemingly taking forever. When the sound and movement

stopped, we crawled out of a locomotive—now leaning at a forty-five degree angle—and checked for wounds. It was a miracle that neither the train crew nor the semi-truck driver and partner were killed or badly injured. I was bruised and beaten up and really shaken and said to myself, *Carol, if you don't get on the next train, you won't stay with it.* I took my next train assignment.

"Way back when, the engines weren't insulated. They had poor heat systems, poor windows, poor visibility, toadstool seats—just all kinds of things. It wasn't conducive for comfort in any way. You had to dress very very warm—several layers so you could peel and then put it back on if you needed to as the weather warmed up. We carried duct tape to seal the windows. You had to climb down into the nose of the train to use the facilities.

"Today they're insulated; they're sound-proofed; the seats are wonderful; the floor is cushioned; they're air-conditioned; good central heat and air; great visibility and doors that locked. Computers tell you everything you need to do and everything you need to know.

"Back then we had a speedometer and we used our watches. We had to time our speed to determine if we were going the right speed for our train. Now they can tell exactly where you're located with GPS. It's so sophisticated. They're running with a lot more horsepower than we did so you have to be a little more careful about notching out, notching down, slack action, one thing and another—but it's much better than it used to be.

"After years of experience I knew the location of all the ice cream shops on the route. If we were delayed, it was a chance for the brakeman to make a fast run before the signal turned green. Fast Freddy's at Gibbon had ready-to-go pizza too.

"A serious incident happened at the Summit in Omaha, not too far from the Missouri River. We stopped our grain train on the hill, set the air brakes and cut away to go into a siding to pick up 50 more cars of grain. Suddenly our parked train on the main line was rolling toward the river. I called the control tower reporting we would try to catch it. They lined the derail switch just in case we didn't. The head brakeman gave a backup sign and the chase was on! As the engineers across the river gave me support and suggestions over the radio, we slowly gained speed to 10 mph, then 20. At 30 mph we made the joint. Now we were tied to a giant running down a hill and heading for the derail. Could we slow it down before the derail? At about 7 mph I considered bailing off, but I said a prayer, decided to ride it out, and continued braking. I stopped just short of derailing.

"Before departing Council Bluffs I had reported an unauthorized person on the fourth unit. Investigation revealed that the rider apparently heard us report him and dropped back a few cars and turned an angle cock in revenge. It prevented proper brake application on the grain cars. His bedroll was found in the end platform of a grain car.

"All the guys and I got along great. It's a different type of relationship. I can tell you stories about fishing and hunting and car remodeling and building houses—all the stories they would tell me. They weren't interested in stories about cooking or sewing or that kind of stuff so it was kind of one-sided, but I did enjoy them. On more than one occasion they shared a heart-wrenching story of a marriage breaking. It is hard on 'rails' to be absent from their family. We are paid well, have wonderful retirement and insurance benefits, but we miss so many of our family activities, those school programs, birthdays, and special events. It was more than once that our Christmas was one or two days before or after the twenty-fifth. We did have the privilege of laying off a trip, but with two round trips per week, it was a big chunk out of the paycheck when we missed a trip. Engineers are paid by the mile.

"It's different working in a man's world than it is in a woman's world. If the men get upset with you, they might bawl you out and it's over. They don't hold grudges. It's done. You move on. You work together the next trip and everything's fine. Women are a little more petty. They don't forget.

"My husband John was very supportive. He'd worked on the railroad and he knew it would be difficult for me. We have two sons: Tim was five and Jim ten, when I started my career. There was a bit of complaining from the children at first, especially about their dad's cooking, but the older they got—when they could drive their own car and they had a charge account down at Young's Sporting Goods—it didn't make much difference. As long as they had the food they needed and clothes in the closet, they just took it in stride. In years to come they were glad. It helped pay for college; it helped play for ski trips; it helped pay for all kinds of things.

"The grandparents were a godsend. Grandpa John and Dorothy took them to school and their home was a safe house after school. Still, as a woman, it's hard to go off and leave your kids. If they're sick or not feeling well your maternal instincts grab you.

"Vacation is totally seniority based. When your children are young you don't have a prayer of being home with them when you really want to be. We just planned our holidays before or after the holiday and made it as special as we could.

"My son Tim has followed in my footsteps and is an engineer running west. He's been out there about 20 years.

"I made many trips to Council Bluffs, Fremont, Missouri Valley and to Marysville. I got to see all the seasons change and watch the harvest. I got excited when somebody painted their house a different color. I loved blowing the whistle and running the little piggies alongside the track in the field. It was a good life. The only thing that was hard was the 24/7—never knowing when you're going and always having to be sure you were rested and ready.

"There were several experiences of tragedy that haunt one for a lifetime. Bearing down on a stalled car, crew members feel helpless. There is nothing that can be done but blow the whistle and pray that a car can make it into the clear. It can take a mile to stop a heavy train. Sadly alcohol played a factor in the senseless death of a teenager I struck.

"Accidents on two occasions were suicidal deaths. I still have a lasting memory of one man stepping in front of my train, adjusting the bill of his hat, and then looking me straight in the eyes as he died in front of me.

"Another stopped his car on the crossing and just waited for me to hit him. My most tragic memory is of a little boy, just a toddler, with a blue hoodie, about two years old who had wandered onto the tracks. There was nothing I could do. That little boy had been removed by track workers from playing on the tracks before—a boy just like the ones I had raised. That's very traumatic and very, very, very hard to get over. With the Lord's help I was able to work my way through all of that, and even though I have the memories, they don't haunt me as much as in past years. I have learned to deal with it; you just have to realize that it's not your fault.

"Early days they didn't have resources to help you work through this and the local newspapers would publish the names of the crew. It took quite a bit of work to convince the media not to publish the crew names for something they had no control over. Their families were already suffering from the tragedy. Operation Lifesaver is a program that has educated the public about rail safety.

"The ranks of women engineers are increasing. There were an estimated 27 nationwide when I began my career—five years later, nearly 40.

"As one of the first in service I received a lot of attention from the news media. On one trip I had a news reporter on board. As we sped along, what a surprise to see a helicopter hovering above our engine with a photographer leaning out the door.

"I caught a passenger special to Omaha with a load of VIPs and the board of directors. There were no complaints about my train handling, and that was good news. After our stop at Fox Park, it made my day to see the directors pointing out the new woman engineer coming down the ladder. That was neat!

"My 32 years of employment was both challenging and rewarding. I am thankful I had the opportunity to work for America's greatest railroad and for the benefits of good pay, insurance and retirement. I am most thankful for the respect and friendship of my peers."

Edwina (Curly) Justus

Edwina Justus began her career with Union Pacific in 1973 as a clerk in Omaha and retired as an engineer out of North Platte in 1998.

"I'd been down to UP in the 60s. I couldn't even get in the door. They weren't taking applications from black people. When an old school friend told me he was working at Union Pacific I said, 'Why don't you see if you can get me on?'

"I was working with Family and Child Services when I got the call to come down to the office to take the test. I passed it on the spot and I was hired. That was 1973. When I started, there was just very few of us black women. At the time, the whole thing was about money. I started out at UP working as a clerk making as much money as the supervisor I was working for at Family and Child Services.

"I was the first black little child that went to Brown Park School in South Omaha. I remember dragging this little kitty home that I found, this little stray cat. It was the only friend that I had. We lived in South Omaha until I started first grade. My dad's mom and my mom's mom lived in north Omaha so we moved to north Omaha.

"Most of the jobs that I had, there were very few of us out there. To go into a place where it's predominantly white men is something I had done before when I started working out at Western Electric. I did that from 1962 until about 1969. You go into a situation where there are men that know black women as one kind of woman, like women of the street, or somebody's maid or something, but not an intellectual kind.

"I started to bid on jobs. I worked my way up. I did jobs I didn't have any idea what the heck I was doing. I just went for it, you know? And I looked the part, because every day I was downtown I could go shopping. I was known as the fashion plate.

"I was working as a traction motor clerk and one day I said, 'I'd like to see what a real engine looks like.' Next thing I know we went around the shops and they showed me what a traction motor was—not that I knew any more than I did in the first place.

"I got up on the engine and asked the guy that was up there with me, 'How do you run one of these things?' There wasn't anything up there but a reverser lever and one that had numbers on it from one to eight. I said, 'I guess that's for your speed. Is that all there is to it?'

"And he said, 'Yeah.'

"I said, 'Well I could do that.'

"He said, 'Why don't you go ahead and put your application in?'

"So a couple of days later I put in my application for locomotive engineer. I thought that was really cute. It was different, you know.

"Two or three months later, I got a call. 'There's a job opening in North Platte for a locomotive engineer, can you be there by...'

"I said, 'No.' I didn't want to go out there. I didn't want that job. White people didn't want to go out there. Nobody wanted to go to North Platte. I bet you could count the people on one hand that left Omaha for any job to go to North Platte because, you know, it's a little dinky town.

"Back when I was a clerk doing all these waybills I could just imagine all these little towns that I'd never heard of before—North Platte was one of them. I could just see this train going by and there are two houses here and a couple of houses on that side of the street. I just couldn't imagine me doing such a thing. I'd never been away from home. I'd never been away from my mother—ever. I'd never lived away from home.

"I talked to my dad. I said, 'They're calling me. They want me to go out to North Platte to take this job as an engineer.'

"He said, 'Take that job.'

"My husband was working at Kellogg's then. Oh, he was so excited about it. I wasn't excited about it because moving was not something I wanted to do. I liked where I was. I liked my dressing up every day and playing make-believe. I didn't want to leave my friends. I just didn't want that job, you know?

Edwina (Curly) Justus – First Black Woman Engineer in Nebraska

"But I went. I went on a freight train of all things. With all my stuff. I rode on the front end—that was the only place there was to ride. The seats were hard. It was in the middle of the night. I was tired. I wasn't seeing anything because it was dark. It was a 13 or 14-hour trip on this freight train because they would go pick up cars...and set out cars... and pick up cars...and set out cars...and stop and wait for other trains to go by. I'm thinking, This is not the life for me.

"When we got to North Platte they let us off at the freight office and there was an audience. I had my hair in rollers. They're like, 'What is this?'

"I stayed in a motel on the north side. They picked me up to take me to the classes out at the yard office. They all had on coveralls. That was just not my environment. That was just not me.

"I worked about three or four weeks before I came home for the first time. I remember laying down on the floor one night. I was just sobbing. I didn't want to go to work. My son, he was twelve or thirteen, he said, 'Mom, I'm going out there with you. I'll take care of you.' But they were going to be running into different circumstances too because there weren't that many black kids that were their ages. There were some families that had been in North Platte since the forties, but they accepted whatever their role was—that they were going to

be called names. That was just the way it was.

"One evening while I was working as a hostler I was out there filling out my time slip and this guy comes in. He says, 'Is the nigger workin' tonight?' And I'm not used to this kind of stuff. When he comes in and sees me, he just gives me this look and he leaves. There were nights when I would be on the floor crying because I didn't want to go back out there because the guys didn't want to work with me.

"After that incident, I started having guys pulling little tricks. They'd put ketchup in my shoes if I left my locker open. They'd tell me to do something and it would be the wrong thing to do— just all kinds of harassing kinds of things. I got to the place where I would just cry before I would go to work. I did not want to go back.

"I worked from May 1976 until February 1977 as a hostler and then went to engineers' training school in Cheyenne. I made my student runs in the third district going west. I became a qualified engineer when I was 34. I was the only black woman engineer in the Union Pacific system. When I moved into the second district I had to make more student runs. It was exciting. I was always ready to roll. It's all been the work of the good Lord. I don't know what I've done to deserve it.

"I went on student trips with some of the older guys. Truckers would come to the hotel we stayed in in Cheyenne. It was wild. They'd have these Cheyenne Days. They'd ride horses all inside the hotel. One time this trucker was sitting there. He pointed to his wallet and he looked at me a couple of times. When I caught on to what he was talking about, I went over to him and said, 'You know, I am so flattered that you would pick me, but you know, I work for the railroad and I make more money than you do.'

"My aunt would tell me, 'Why don't you wear those coveralls, you know, I thought you had to wear those striped coveralls with the engineer's hat.'

"I said, 'We don't dress like that anymore.' She was so disappointed. When I would go to the schools to give presentations, I'd put on them coveralls. That's what they imagined from all the books that engineers looked like.

"At the time we moved to North Platte there was a trucking company and the bus ran out there. Sutherland was building that power plant. There was a big influx of new people that were coming into North Platte. In the late seventies or early eighties, a lot of those things left. A lot of places just didn't have the work anymore. We helped some people get on the railroad, but they were people that didn't like that kind of work, so they didn't stay out there.

"Living in North Platte, I learned so much. I can't tell you the number of lives that I touched, or touched mine, during the time that I was out there."

The North Platte Telegraph wrote an article about Curly in January of 1983. In it she says, "I sometimes feel like I'm a missionary here to educate others about what black people are like." At that time the population of North Platte was 22,605: 20,994 were white; 79 were black.

Diane Pfortmiller

"I loved working for the railroad. They treated me well and it helped me to raise my children on a good wage. I started as a clerk and worked all the jobs available in the office as much as I could. I was transferred to engine service and hostled power for nine years in Bailey Yard. I was promoted to locomotive engineer and worked the switch engine for several years. I also worked the 'Branch' (North Platte to Gering/South Morrill) and Cheyenne on the road handling coal trains, auto racks, soda ash, double stacks, etc. All total over 23 years.

"I was one of the first women hired in transportation. I would've been the first being hired off the street, but I turned it down wanting an office job and thinking women didn't belong in the 'field'! We can do a man's job and do it just as well. Some of them have a problem with us taking a man's job away from him, but some of us also had families to raise ourselves. It is hard work, sometimes difficult, but rewarding."

Deborah D. Dancer Tanner

"I started working for the railroad in 1977. I was one of the first two women to be hired in the transportation department. It was the time of the equal opportunity employment. I was hired to be a switchman—or switchperson—or there's another name that's not quite so endearing that the gentlemen called me until they got to know me better.

"I remember my very first pay trip. It was midnight and it's dark. I was supposed to work at the old hump. I started out in plenty of time. I thought I was going to just drive right to it. I could not find the old hump. I drove every road I could think of. At that time there were lots of roads out there with no lights. I was finally in tears. I drove over to the Barn Store and called Gary Lang who was my manager that night. I was bawling. 'I can't find the hump, Gary, please I'm going to get into trouble and it's my first trip. Please come and get me. Help me find the hump.' He just started laughing. He finally says, 'Go across the road and go across the track. Just sit there and wait for me. I will come and get you.' He came and met me and led me to the hump.

"I worked in the yards putting trains together, switching boxcars around, throwing switches—doing everything that the men were doing. I will say I was not received well because I was a woman. I'm weaker. There's no way I was going to be able to do the jobs that they were doing. Until I proved myself I put up with a lot of lip—derogatory statements to my face and behind my back.

"We did flat switching. Each of us stood at a switch for a different track. The engine pushed cars toward us. One person would run next to the cars to grab the handle that opened up the coupler. They'd say, 'Kick it, kick it, kick it.' There might be three or four cars rolling all at the same time. Here they come. You're leaning down and you throw the switch over and the car goes into that track. There might be one behind it that is going straight so soon as those wheels cleared. You grabbed the switch handle to throw it back. It was fun! It was a blast! It was my favorite job.

"I don't know if they still have to run with the cars to unhook them. I haven't been out there since

1987. I hurt my hand pulling up on a handle. I didn't get my strength back in that wrist. That was the end of my railroad career.

"There were some real bugger switches that nobody could throw easily. If there was a switch I couldn't throw—and when I say throw a switch, I mean you grabbed a handle and pulled and that moved the points of the rail—I would say, 'I can't do that. Would one of you come down and do that?' It was usually a switch that even they couldn't throw. That was a kind of leverage thing for me.

"I didn't have any trouble with the management as a woman. It was mostly just the men that were used to a man's world.

"I will say there were no bathrooms. That had to be addressed. I remember the old yard office. The bathroom was just a dump. It was just hideous. Our lunchroom was right there in this big room also. There were like big long picnic tables. I mean it was just grody. It was dirty. It was gray and ugly. It was awful.

"There was a job where you had to work down in the bowl. There are like 60 some tracks. Down at the end of the bowl was a tiny little shack. It was like the old three-holer outhouse—that's how small it was. There was a seat in there and that was about it. You'd sit down there by yourself with your radio all night long to take radio transmissions from the engines to the east of you that were putting trains together.

"One time they wanted me to look for a rail stretcher. I was outside walking around the shack seeing if it was leaning up against the wall. I'm going, 'Ok, what's it look like?' Then I could hear them just yuk-yuk-yuking. Of course, it's like snipe hunting.

"They have these real tall highlights out there. In the summer they drew the June bugs. I'm not a bug person. June bugs are the worst things that God ever made. They're sticky. They're hard-shelled. They make noise. They're just gross. We were working over on the north end of the bowl. There are lots of highlights. The boys sent me down into the bowl to couple up some cars. It's nighttime. The lights are shining bright. I'm walking down between the boxcars looking for hoses that need to be coupled, not realizing that the June bugs are coming off the lights onto the tops of the boxcars and then they're falling off the boxcars. It was warm. I had a t-shirt on. The first second that I felt a June bug going down my neck I screamed bloody murder. That shirt came off so fast. I mean I was shaking it. I was hopping around like I was on hot coals. I wasn't the least bit

Deb Dancer

embarrassed because those bugs were on me. They just laughed. Nobody ever said a word.

"I remember working a midnight. It's cold. I'm walking in the bowl. You're always walking in the bowl out there. I saw a caboose. I thought, *You know what? I'm gonna get on this caboose and warm up a little bit. At least get out of the wind and the cold.* I walked in and there sat a hobo. He was taking cigarettes out of the little ashtray at the table where the conductors sit and do their paperwork. He was taking the tobacco and rolling his own cigarettes. I nearly had a heart attack. I'm by myself. I'm a woman. I'm little. And this guy was pretty good size. He looked up and I said, 'Well, I was just checking this car. I guess I'll go.' I backed out. That was kind of scary.

"From being a switchman, I got my foreman rights which meant I was the boss of the crew of myself, my two helpers and the engineer. I went to Cheyenne and Denver and Sidney. I remember the dreaded Sidney Local. It was kind of scary. If you haven't ever been on an engine going 65 miles an hour, it's like riding a bucking bronco. You had to sit down and hang on.

"The first time we had to get off the caboose and move cars around, Benny Covington said, 'Ok, come out on the back step. We're gonna get off right up here.' This was back before the train had to come to a full stop for you to get on or off. Benny has really, really long legs. He got off. I mean he just kind of swung his leg down into the ballast and took two steps and he was at a dead stop. Me. I step off that caboose and I'm like run, run, run—I'm running as hard as I can run and I'm praying I don't fall down. I probably ran a quarter of a mile. Then I had to walk back. Oh they laughed. That was so hard. That was a learning experience.

"There was another unpleasant part of riding out on the road—the toilets in the engine nose. Nobody wanted to go there. I guess you do what you have to do.

"Back in the 80s Union Pacific did a television ad campaign. They had an engineer leaning out the window singing, 'We're a great big rolling railroad, hear the diesel engines roar.' People like me sang different sections of the song. It went on and on and on. It was a really cool advertisement.

"My husband started working out at the railroad in 1978. We had a baby boy. If he was home babysitting in the morning while I was working my shift, he would bring the baby. We would meet on the road. He'd pass me the baby through the window and then I would go home and be the babysitter and he would work.

"As time went on more and more women got hired. They were times it was an all woman crew except for the engineer. We did fine. We had no problem getting our work done. Some of the men were not too happy about having a woman boss, but we became friends.

"It was a wonderful experience, it really was, working out there."

Rhonda Putman Steffes Quaney

"I hired on in '79. I was a switchman—well, that's the title we had. My dad was an officer on the railroad at one time. When he found out I was getting 'hired on' he told me he didn't want me to work out there...and that I wouldn't like it. He knew that being a switchman was a physically demanding and somewhat dangerous job.

"I was 22. I was only thinking that I needed a good paying job.

"Don Crago was in charge of hiring. I went out to the office many times saying, 'I want a job. I want a job.' I think he finally gave me a job to get rid of me. He probably didn't think I would be able to do the physical part. Back then I only weighed about 110 pounds.

"My class was qualified on 7/9/79. When the big layoffs happened we were some of the first ones that were cut.

"During the time that I was furloughed I got married, had two children and then my husband died in a farm accident. Then I got called back to the railroad. It just happened—boom, boom, boom.

"A lot of people took the buyout or just found other employment. They offered a $5000 buyout and then they offered a $10,000 buyout for a guaranteed (contract) employee.

"Catfish (Ray) Hunter called me and said, 'Don't take the buyout. They're going to start hiring and you're going to have a lot of seniority.' I took his advice and came back. For about a year I was on a switchman's extra board. It was a hard year since my kids were very young.

"When I was hired there were women who did their job in switching and there were women who didn't do the job—like any occupation. I really looked up to Pat Hardy, Deb Tanner, Rita Dobbins, and Linda Rowley. They were all well known for pulling their own weight. They knew what they were doing. I knew that was what I wanted to do—learn the job well.

"When I hired out of course I had no clue what I was doing. I remember being in the old west yard at midnight. The tracks were so close that you could almost touch the cars on both sides. The guys were just jerking the 'trim' out. I was hanging on to this pole thinking, *Ok. I'm gonna die down here.* I wish I could remember the name of the guy who came across me and told me, 'I'm going teach you how to get on and off of fast moving equipment.' He told me, 'Run as fast as you can and when it feels right, jump!' Pretty soon I got good at it. A good engineer would rip out the trim and roll in the slack to slow down just enough that you could bail off safely.

"One night I was near cab alley (where they spotted cabooses) having trouble with a drawbar that was jammed on an auto rack. Scott Ziegler, a seasoned switchman, was like, 'You don't have to be 200 pounds to get these.' He showed me how to take the knuckle out and how to hit it to get it unjammed and how you could use your butt and legs to move the drawbar instead of lifting with the front and trying to scooch it over and hurting your back.

"When we were first hired, we still had the van yards. That's where we did a lot of flat-switching. They won't even do that type of switching now. Back then, they'd put you on a cut of cars—it might be 3 cars, it might be a cut of 25 cars—and they'd 'drop you'. They'd go really fast and they'd drop you down into these tracks. You'd have to tie enough hand brakes to get the free rolling cut of cars to quit moving before they went out on the main line on the other end.

"One of their notorious tricks, which I did not know at the time, was to put somebody, especially a rookie, on a very heavy cut of cars. Then they'd just fly you down there. Of course it's sloping downhill. Well, some people couldn't put on enough hand brakes to stop it from going out, and then you could get fired.

"They dropped me with—I don't know what kind of cars they were. All I know is the first three hand brakes didn't touch it. I just kept having to run and catch another car and catch another car. I think they were putting bets on me. I did get it stopped, but I was mad. It was very dangerous.

"When I was hired it was kind of the end of the old school railroad. They still had three people on each crew and they still had cabooses on the train. There was no woman's bathroom for years. You pretty much had to say, 'I'm going in. If you come in, I'll scream.'

"Computers came in the later 1980s and things really started to change. It started transitioning with the new construction of the west yard. Eventually they stopped letting people get on or off moving equipment and added safety equipment like ear protection.

"There were a lot of jobs you could hold. There were two humps, two trim yards and the van yards—and cab alley back in that day they still had cabooses. Or you could be down in the bowl helping crews hook up cars to get their trains out faster. That was called a 'longfielder'. For a time they also forced us to cover hostling jobs at the diesel shop hostling power. If you were working the extra board, you could catch any one of those jobs on any of three shifts. That board turned fast. It was not unusual to be called back to work in eight hours. I was really glad when I had enough seniority to hold a regular job with set hours.

"Some guys were arrogant. But most of them were down to earth and willing to work as a team. Actually some us worked together often enough that we were good friends and made it fun.

"As far as I know I was the first woman to qualify on the fourth district as a conductor. Also at one point they wanted swtichmen to get engineer qualified. They only had so many women out there and they needed a woman in each engineer class. They offered to let me run around quite a few men to qualify as an engineer

Rita Dobbins, Deb Tanner, Rhonda Quaney (photo courtesy of Christy Callendar)

just because I was a woman. The guys were mad about that, and rightfully so. Everything with the railroad is about seniority. I ended up turning it down because I was raising two kids. It was better for me to be in the yard and have a five-day a week schedule.

"When I went in to sign the paper refusing it, the officer handling the paper work told me I was a fool. It was a hard choice, but in 1993, I was able to take a buyout that was only offered to switchmen. At the end of my railroad career I was mostly in the tower working as a foreman with the computers. That was the advantage of having seniority.

"What advice would I give to a woman today? Just be yourself. If you have common sense and a good work ethic you can make a good living and be an asset to the company. Even though I once said that I would never be a railroader or marry one, I'm proud to be a third generation railroader, married to a third generation railroader. It was an honor to have been able to work in the transportation department, in a job that was not traditionally held by women. Being a switchman was challenging, fun, and supported my family well. I hope I'm remembered as someone who worked hard and was good at her job."

Rita Aylward Dobbins

"I was hired out on the railroad in June of '78 as a switchman. I worked in the yards. I built trains to send out on the road. I wore steel-toed boots and jeans with a belt loop so I could carry the radio. The year it was so snowy—'79? '80?—I wore my pack boots it seemed like for six months. I was laid off— furloughed—in October of '81 in that big layoff.

"I was working at a retail store in downtown North Platte. Linda Rowley (Smith now) came into the store. She said, 'They're hiring women out at the railroad. Think that's something we could do? They need so many women in each class.'

"And I'm thinking, *You know that might be kind of fun.* So we went out. They hired us right there on the spot to be in the class.

"We heard that you had to pass a physical to hire on to the UP. Usually the physical was the first thing you did even before the classes started but because they needed two women for the class, the physical came last. We had classroom time first. I studied all week long and wasn't sure that I'd pass. It was tough. I was out of my element. I didn't know what all it entailed. I probably studied harder for that test than any high school class

that I'd ever studied for. I passed, then I had to pass the medical portion.

"We passed the book portion and then we had to go out onto the train and learn the physical part of the job. Bob Sparks and Don Abegg taught us the right and wrong way to get on and off the engine and cars, how to tie hand brakes, and how to line switches.

"Once you qualified in all the categories, you took student trips to each job station in the UP yards. Once qualified, you were added to the working extra board.

"The first night I was called by the dispatcher to go to work, I was a nervous wreck. Linda and I both were called to work the west hump. For this job the engineer pushes the train to the hump hill. The switchman walks along the train pulling pins on the cars to let them go over the hill down into the bowl. Our engineer was Darrell Marquardt. He was so great. Oh my God, I was so nervous, but Darrell took very good care of us. We survived the first night.

"Once we got past that point it was just another day at the office. It was a very interesting job and usually something new every day. I really enjoyed the time I worked for UP. It was a very physical job but helped me keep in shape. The jobs I worked included a lot of walking.

"What I liked best about my job was that you went out, you did your work, and you went home. There wasn't any drama—rarely any drama. I liked working out there. I came from a ranching community so working on equipment or working outside was just something I was used to. I guess that's why I liked it so much.

"I worked in the old yard where they still had the freight house and the van yards. It was a little nerve-racking in the afternoons when the mail trains would come in and we'd have to switch those out running beside the cars pulling pins and throwing switches on foot. They don't do that anymore due to safety reasons.

"In doing flat-switching, they gave you a list of cars and where the cars needed to go. Pretty much what I got in on was switching out the mail trains. The mail came in and you'd have to have it done by a certain time so the train could make its next destination. That got pretty hectic and pretty involved. You wanted to be on a crew that knew what it was doing. The van yards were actually semi-trailers on flat cars and the semi-trailers were full of mail, etc. If you threw the wrong switch or pulled the wrong pin on the cars, the process was slowed down and I didn't want to be the woman slowing down the job.

"Trimming refers to a train that you're building. You have several different tracks. You have to go in and couple up cars, create your train, hook it together, pull it back, shove it into another track, hook it up, pull it back. Sometimes there might be a car you'd have to set out. Flat-switching, building a train and trimming is similar terminology. It might mean different things at different locations.

"There was a right and a wrong way to get off a moving car. You definitely didn't want to get off the wrong way because it would slap you to the ground in a hurry. There were great engineers that would really slow down for you to get on, give you that little bit of time to grab and go. Ray Maxwell was a good one. I remember working with him.

"There were crews that kind of worked together all the time. We'd bring food. Somebody would bring a grill. Somebody'd bring the salad. Somebody'd bring dessert. Somebody would bring steaks or hamburgers and we'd grill out on the unit. It was really fun. I don't think that would go over so good now. It was a great thing back then. Everybody wanted to be on our crew because we had good food.

"I never had any problems working with the guys. If you could do your job, you never really had any trouble. If there was a switch that I just really couldn't do, I'd give it all I could. If I couldn't do it, someone would have to get off the unit and help. I didn't want to be known as the girl who always needed help. But sometimes if a switch needed an adjustment it would be very hard to throw. So if a man struggled with it too I didn't feel so bad.

"When I got laid off the railroad, I took a teller position at Mutual Building and Loan. I started dating my husband. We were engaged when I got called back to work. We talked about me going back onto the railroad full time but worried about layoffs again. I really liked my job at the bank. I didn't know if I wanted to work out at the railroad being married. There was rumor of a buyout about that time.

"At that time you could work so many days per work half to keep your seniority. I worked in the yards on the weekends to keep my seniority. Then they came along with the buyout. I took that big $5000 buyout. I bought a car. At the time it seemed like the right thing to do.

"Probably the hardest part of working out there was the winter. The winters seemed to last forever. During the winter months I could only hold a midnight job and of course that is the coldest time. You had to be out in it. If you had to push cars down the track, you had to be on that lead car to protect the shove and you were shoved right into the snow if it was stormy. You had to dress for it. I always found it better to put on a lot of layers. It was easier to take off layers than wishing I'd brought them to work with me.

"What advice would I give to a woman today? Just do your job. Do what's asked of you.

"It was a good experience for me. Now my husband works for Union Pacific. I can really relate to his hours, his frustrations of working odd hours, never being able to plan anything and when he talks about work I understand what he is talking about. At our household we just kind of go with the flow. I think that's why our marriage has been so great because I understand his job and the weird hours.

"I always admired Pat Hardy Heinzle, Deb Dancer Tanner, and Rhonda Putman Quaney for staying with Union Pacific as long as they did. I enjoyed working with them when I could. Once in a while we had an all women switching crew and I'm sure not one car went on the ground that shift. Thanks for the memories, ladies!"

Shirley Mitchell Tuenge

"I worked for the Lincoln County Judge's Office in North Platte, Nebraska, before hiring out to Union Pacific Railroad. My decision to hire out was influenced by wanting to improve my life financially.

"I was also inspired by my family's railroad history. My stepfather Lyle Miller was a director/superintendent at the diesel shop and other locations. He gets credit for mentoring me about the railroad industry. My biological father Bill Mitchell was a locomotive diesel machinist. My grandfather Harry Mitchell was a locomotive engineer who ran west out of North Platte to Sidney or Sterling in freight/passenger service. My sister Bonny Branting is a carman. All of them have inspired me on my 'railroading'.

"I tried for some time to get hired, thinking it probably wouldn't happen, but persistence paid off. In 1977 I was hired as the first woman switchman in North Platte.

"Working in a male-dominated industry has been a challenge. I remember when I first started. On a couple of occasions when I reported to work with a switchcrew, a few male co-workers would call a relief (have the railroad call another switchman in to fill his job), refusing to work with a woman.

"You have to show interest in learning the job and proving yourself to your co-workers. Act like a lady and most of the time you are treated like one. Don't take the job too personal; give and take a little; just be yourself. Keep an open mind— that makes a difference.

"Switching/train crew service training teaches you to move trains safely in the yards and over the road. You climb ladders, board cars and engines, operate track switches, inspect cars, and use radio communications to control train movement.

"I'm very short. I thought, *How am I going to board moving cars?* My mind-set was it's like jumping rope. You know how you run in at the right time? That's how I got on a moving car. Now they stop cars and engines to board up. It's much more safety-minded at Union Pacific now.

"I had conductor rights running east to Council Bluffs, Fremont, and Marysville. Later I was set up as first woman yardmaster at North Platte. Duties included direct supervision of the yard's many employees and the facilitation of the movement of freight trains and engines in and out of the yards efficiently and safely.

"In 1979 I transferred to Cheyenne where I entered into engine service. I worked at the Cheyenne roundhouse hostling road, switch and Amtrak engines.

"Later I worked the third district (North Platte to Cheyenne, Denver and South Morrill) as a promoted engineer. Most road trips are about the same, although I will always remember one that was different.

"I was a fireman with a Denver crew going towards Denver. We were going around a curve and up ahead we saw something long and shiny and someone waving 'stop' at us. Our first thought was, *It's a gas transport!* Quite frightening! The semi-truck and trailer was stalled on the railroad tracks. The head brakeman radioed back to the rear-end crew (conductor and rear brakeman) about the situation.

"Getting closer, we whistled off a lot and dynamited (dumped) the air brakes trying to stop the train. It takes a while for a train to stop. We were dropping speed—35 miles per hour—but not stopping.

"Finally the engineer said, 'We gotta jump off!'

"Out the back locomotive door we went and ducked underneath the handrail. We jumped off and landed in the right-of-way ditch. Luckily I didn't break any bones. I was scraped up a lot and very sore for a while. I was young. That helped. The two gentlemen on the head-end with me had some broken bones and one had a head contusion. We were lucky!

Shirley Tuenge

"The train hit the semi—lo and behold it was a milk transport! We didn't know. If it was a gas transport, we wouldn't have made it out alive. It was a mess, but at least there were no fatalities.

"Several years later I stayed home to raise a family, then went back to work in the car department. This department is a whole different side to the railroad. I didn't realize that there are so many parts to a freight car. I'm still learning every day. Recently I was promoted to a car foreman (management).

"There's a lot of terminology out there. Dynamite the train means to throw the emergency brake. A really old term for it is big hole. Your older engineers would have said, 'Big hole the train.' That means you're gonna dump it just to get it stopped. Throw it into emergency. I still hear the term dynamite out there. As a car foreman I might get a report that there's a dynamiter on one of the cars. That means one of my air valves is stuck. It's not releasing the brakes like it should so you're going to be dragging a car with its brakes on. They call it a dynamiter meaning the brakes are set and won't release.

"And say you've got a speed clearance to go sixty miles an hour. Somebody creeps up to sixty-five or seventy, they're high-spotting. That's what they always called it.

My granddad helped me. He'd tell me about handling the train, like how to do stretch-braking. Stretch-braking is when you've got the brakes on but you're starting to throttle out. He said, 'By the time you release your brake and have it notch one, your rear wheel on the caboose should be loading.' And it was true. It did. I know because I'd ask conductors to tell me as soon as it started moving. It was smooth. You never want to spill the coffee cup that's back there. Just things like that. The old heads, they know a lot.

"Most of the railroad jobs require that you work on-call, even on weekends and holidays, and in all weather conditions, but I've enjoyed every one of the jobs that I have worked at Union Pacific. My favorite position is locomotive engineer. Train handling is exciting.

"I plan to retire from the Union Pacific, God willing. It's been a challenge, very rewarding and satisfying, and I've loved it. There are many job opportunities and career choices out there. It's a great company with great benefits. I'm glad that more women are getting hired in all departments. I encourage women who want an exciting career in the railroad industry to 'hire out'."

Jody Best

"I started August 14, 1979—right out of high school. I'm still there so in August I'll have 32 years. I'm a switchman in the yard. I went out on the road as a conductor in '89 for about six months but that was enough for me. I've stayed in the yard since then.

"After I hired out I was laid off for six years and didn't get called back until '85. In the meantime I'd gotten married and found other jobs. Then I got called back and I've been out there ever since.

"The most challenging thing about my job is the weather. I'm a fair weather person. I don't like being cold. It gets pretty physical when you have boots and coveralls and your vest and your remote control box and everything weighing you down. Sweeping switches and getting on and off equipment in the winter is challenging. You 'sweep a switch' when you have a switch to hand line and there's snow packed in it. Or it's filled up with water and frozen and you have to chop out the ice.

"I like hot weather except days when it's 100° and you don't have any breeze going on. It gets pretty hot around that equipment. The job used to be more physical but actually it's not too bad any more.

"To hold a good foreman job is pretty tough. You'd think after 32 years I'd be able to, but there are about 23 people ahead of me in seniority and that takes up the foreman jobs in the yard. A lot of times I'm the helper. Probably in the next five years the turnover is going to be good. There are a lot of people retiring. I might be able to be Number One by the time I turn 60. I turn 51 this year so I have nine years to go before I retire. I'll have almost 42 years in by then.

"Switchmen put trains together. Cars go over the east hump or the west hump. They get divided into other tracks. We take cars from one or two or three or four tracks and shove them into a big long forwarding track.

Then crews get on those trains and leave town. When I'm a foreman I get to work inside and run the computers. I look at the cars that are coming up on the screen and tell the helper what to do. That's kind of fun.

"You got to be pretty strong and I don't mean physically. You got to be mentally strong. I work around men every day and there are really no other women out there. You've got to be strong knowing that you're going to be out there with just guys.

"I'm pretty lucky to make the wages I do and to have the insurance I do. It's been really good for my son and me. I encourage women who are going to be out there to be strong, but to be gentle with yourself. Sometimes it gets challenging and you're like, *What am I doing out here? I'm in the snow.* But you know what? It's doable. It really is. And it's a good job. I don't have any regrets being out there all these years.

"After high school a lot of my friends were hiring out on the railroad. I wasn't up for going to college and I just thought, *Oh why not.* I knew a gentleman who worked out there and he got me an interview and I got hired. Fortunately for me, the guys I went to school with were there. They were all pretty good to me. You have the exceptions that don't want women out there, but I work with a great group of guys.

"A couple of years ago I was at a meeting and there were about 100 women. When I hired out in '79, I could count on one hand how many women had been in my department.

"I wear a vest with an RCL (Remote Control Locomotive) to run the locomotives. There are no engineers in the yard now. The engineers and conductors are all out on the road. They went from having a four-person crew—engineer, conductor and two brakemen—to just an engineer and a conductor. A lot of the engineers thought that they were going to stay in the yard forever. When the remote control took over, all the engineers had to go out on the road. They didn't have an option. Sometimes that's tough.

"In the yards we have a foreman and a helper. We both carry remote control boxes that we use to run the locomotives. We pull trains out and cars out and switch out different cars, all with the remote control box.

"You have to be RCL-qualified and you have to have certification rights with you to run the locomotive. We have managers, people who come out and ride with us, and certify us. As far as being an engineer who goes out on the road, I'm not qualified in that way. Just with the remote control.

Jody Best wearing a RCL (Remote Control Locomotive)

"Engineers used to say they run the locomotive by the seat of their pants because they could feel how heavy it was when they were running the locomotive. When I first started I was like, *I'm never going to be able to do this.* We all thought we were never going to be able to feel this stuff like a real engineer. It was tough getting used to it. After about a year or so though, we started feeling like we were kind of running the locomotive virtually by the seat of our pants. We can feel it if we're on the locomotive or if we're on the car, but even if we're not, we can hear the locomotive. We've gotten used to how it sounds when you're pulling out a heavy train versus a light train.

"It's been a lot of adjusting running the locomotive. It's kind of fun. It's scary sometimes to know that you are the only one who's in control of those locomotives and all those cars.

"The RCL box weighs six pounds. There are days it gets heavy or it gets really hot because we have to wear a full vest that buttons up the sides, plus we have a radio that we have to carry. In the wintertime, that's when the weight comes on because you got coveralls and snow boots. In the summertime it's not so bad. You always have to wear reflective gear on the outside of your body that goes 360 degrees around.

"The RCL hooks on our vest. You have little knobs that you use to direct the locomotive and to stop it and start it. It's like one of those remote control cars that you drive around. There are 10 to 12 knobs. Certain knobs make the engine go. You learn how to use it and how to ramp it down, just like an engineer does with controls in the locomotive. There's a lot of safety built into it. Our maximum speed is only 10 mph.

"If I'm at the point of the move and my helper is farther away, and I need to get the remote to him, I have a button on my box which we call a pitch. I say, 'Pitch is in the air.' My helper pushes a different knob and then he's got control of the locomotive. It's pitch and catch.

"If you're a foreman, you're the A. If you're a helper, you're the B. If I'm A, I say, '3402B, pitch is in the air.' He'll catch it and he'll click a button and it'll say, '3402B consist ready.' It tells us who has the pitch and who doesn't. We do it over the radio because a lot of times we're not face-to-face. We could be two cars away or we could be 100 cars away. Somebody always has to be on the point of the locomotive. The point is the head end of the move. He has to be in control of the move if he's on the point. Backward or forward, you have to protect that point. If I'm on some cars and I'm shoving in my direction I have to be in control. If we have to go back the other way, I pitch it to my helper and he has to be in control of the movement in his direction.

"There are days in any job that you tend to cuss it a bit, but over the last few years I've learned to appreciate my job. I think maybe it's that I'm getting older—or knowing there are so many people laid off in other jobs and other areas. I'm very blessed to have the job that I have.

"My son Thomas is 24. Fortunately I was in a position where I could take time off when he needed me around or was out of school and sick. A lot of jobs that's pretty tough to do.

"I went through the midnight phase and the afternoon phase out there and now I work Monday through Friday on daylights. That's one good thing about the seniority—daylights. It's tough out there sometimes, it is. There's a lot that goes on. It can be pretty humbling too. But I've enjoyed it.

Management

Donna Fair

"I had a very close friend, Doretta Kleinkauf. She worked at the railroad and recommended me. They called me probably ten years before I came to the railroad. I didn't go at that time because my son was just starting kindergarten.

"I worked with Waneita Schomer in the car department when I went on board in '75. The first day she called me and wanted to know if I knew where it was.

"I said, 'No.'

"She said, 'I'll meet you at the Barn Store. You can follow me in.' I followed her in and that was my first day. Nice, nice lady.

"To begin with, I was hired as a clerk. I had all clerical duties. I typed the daily report of the units in the diesel shop and various reports like personal injuries. I was very interested in safety so I asked if I could do a weekly posting regarding personal injuries and safety and was given permission to do so. That was fun. I replaced the chief clerk when he was transferred.

"In 1984 I transferred from mechanical to transportation where I stayed until I took the buy-out in 1994. I was Manager Administration and Purchasing in the transportation department. The difference between the mechanical and transportation departments is like night and day. The mechanical deals with the mechanical end of the railroad—with the locomotives. Transportation is strictly your transportation crews.

I was the head of the clerical. I enjoyed tremendously everything I did. I can't say I preferred one over the other. I am a people person. I loved the people I worked with and for. It was just a tremendous oppor-

tunity as far as I'm concerned. I enjoyed every minute of it.

"The diesel shop was where my father was a pipefitter for 45 years. He worked at the roundhouse. He retired in 1968 and they opened the new diesel shop in 1971. My father loved the railroad. That's what I heard all my life—railroad. To begin with they didn't know me by name; they knew me as Cleo Miller's daughter, which was fine with me. It was a blessing to me. I can honestly say that in my total time working with the railroad, working in the man's world, so to speak, I never had any problem with any of the gentlemen that I worked with.

"My hours were variable. As a manager, you're on call 24/7, so you raise your children a lot by telephone. I was head of drug testing. There were many times I was on board at 4:00 A.M. to get everything done that I had to and I might be there at 8 o'clock at night yet. They asked me to be Nebraska's first lady engineer. That was before Carol Townsend. I chose at that time not to because of my children. I would have had to have somebody live in my home to get the children to school and to be on call, so I didn't take it. My children were very young when I started.

"If you're a single parent that's awfully hard. There's a lot of guilt. Missing all their school stuff, you know. My mother always worked, and I always said that I wasn't going to because I wanted to be part of their lives, but you gotta do what you gotta do. I did miss a lot of their school stuff.

"Here's an example of what you have to contend with when you have children and you work: I had a telephone call one day. My daughter was crying.

Donna Fair (photo courtesy of Christy Callendar)

"She said, 'Donny's bleeding.' (Donny was her brother.)

"I said, 'Why is Donny bleeding?'

"She said, 'Because I hit him over the head with a hammer.'

"So I said, 'I'm on my way.'

"That's what you contend with when you're a mother.

"I missed many of the school activities that a mother should enjoy, but I had to provide. Getting the kids to school was a hardship. I lived way on the east end of town. The school's on the west end. When my daughter was going to junior high, I had to be to work. Sometimes my mother and father helped me, but in later years, I couldn't find anybody who lived on the east end that I could pay to take my daughter to school. I took her to the rec center. She stayed there until she could go to the school. It was right next to it. Then the rec center called me. My daughter loved to talk. There was a problem with her talking so much. I thought, Oh what am I gonna do? I did take her there for a while after that.

"I save everything railroad-connected. I've been collecting railroad stuff continually. I have things at home yet that I have not yet taken to my office. My connection now with the railroad is my Office Service. I do mainly railroad retirements and disability, which is good for me. It satisfies my connection and love for the railroad. It's something that started when I was working out there and visiting with retired employees that formerly worked there. They would say they didn't have a particular benefit because they didn't know about it when they retired. I have a big problem with that. When a person works thirty years for a company I believe he should have everything he has worked for. That has been the purpose of what I do—to make sure the employee has what he has worked for. The good part of what I do is that I still get to see the people I worked for and with.

"The railroad's my life. When I see a train or something railroad, I grab it to add to my collection.

"The wooden sign on my wall originated at the diesel shop. When the superintendent L. L. Miller was transferred I asked what they were going to do with it. I love wood. In fact I took four years of creative woodwork. They were going to throw it away so I asked if I could have it. I stored it in my garage until I opened this office. Now I use it with my decor of the railroad.

"I have several locks and keys. Some are from when my father worked for the railroad. Employees brought in some. A railroad employee made the clocks. I was given the old lantern as a retirement gift when I left the railroad. I've got a lantern that came from either the Rock Island or the C&W. Some of the lanterns are quite old. Much of this I've accumulated from sales. I have a Union Pacific knife, Union Pacific golf tees, belt buckles, square nails, train whistles, and various pictures of the yard. There's a General Electric locomotive picture that was taken years ago.

"Union Pacific came out with various stuffed bears and I've accumulated them through the years. I have two brass reversers. They don't use brass ones anymore. The little spike with a train on it was purchased from the Golden Spike. There's a train made by a UP employee. The hard hat is mine from working at the diesel shop. Some of this is from when I worked with United Way. I have certificates from training classes, books on the UP, an old rules book, a stoplight, service unit bags, a spacer used on the tracks, and trains all over the office. An FRA inspector made that lantern into a lamp and gave it to me as a gift. Our Christmas tree is our holiday tree. We decorate it according to the holiday. We have more bears. Those little gray ones have been around for quite some time. This rail was made in 1888. It was used on the GI to Hastings section of the St Joe and GI branch of the UPRR.

"We hope to have something very special for Rail Fest. I'm hoping everyone will come in and have a tour—maybe have some coffee and enjoy this with us."

Section IV

Women
of Today

Introduction

Over a century has passed since Minnie McCoy joined Union Pacific in North Platte as a stenographer in 1907. One could argue that the hundreds of women now employed by Union Pacific are the result of two world wars and copious legislation. That would be partially true. War and legislation cleared the tracks, but the change required women (and men) of stamina who were willing to challenge stereotypes.

Our society has evolved from a world where women could not own property but were themselves property, to a place where women are limited only by what they are willing to risk.

It will be inspiring to note what changes women (and men) (and the railroad) concoct during the next hundred years.

A private railroad car is not an acquired taste. One takes to it immediately.

— Eleanor Robson Belmont

Firemen/Oilers

Brenda Hansen

"I started at the railroad in 2004 as a fireman/oiler. I was scared to death because I'd always stayed home with my kids, but I just had to. My husband left and I had five kids to support.

"My kids hated it because they were used to having me at home to go to their ball games and stuff like that, but I talked to them. They realized that's what I had to do to support them; to put a roof over their heads; to pay for doctor bills. Now they like it. They're proud of their mom, especially when they see me in a locomotive bringing it through the shop. And they like the benefits of my job.

"My first duties of the day are to move the fixed locomotives out of the shop and move the broken ones in. We clean the cabs and wash all the windows. We spray the engines down with soap and then spray the soap off with a high-pressure hot water hose. That's pretty much my job. It's pretty simple. Anybody can do it.

"It's challenging to get the locomotives moved in a safe and timely manner so the crews can go to work right away. It can be pretty confusing when you've got to hook into locomotives and set them over to different rails and remember what numbers you've got going where. Sometimes you've got to shuffle and slice and dice—well, they call it making cuts. Put this one here and that one there. Bring this one out of this track and back over into this one. If you've got two or three locomotives sitting in your way you've got to move those. There isn't always a lot of room.

"When I heard the railroad was hiring, I put in my application online. I got a phone call at like 10:30 at night. 'Please come to an interview at 7 o'clock in the morning.' I went and I got hired.

"I'd tell a woman who wanted to work for the railroad, 'If you get hired, do your job. Just do your job. Do what you're out there to do.' There are times you have to ask for help because women don't have the upper body strength that men do. If it's as simple as a trashcan that's got chunks of iron in it, it's heavy. Instead of hurting yourself, ask for help. They're glad to help. That's my advice. Just do your job because that's what you're there for. That's what you get paid for.

"We had a blizzard. I needed to spread salt and sand outside the shop so we didn't have slip and trip hazards. They put me on a forklift with a big ol' pallet of salt and sand. I was out there spreading salt and sand and loving it because I love winter. Another forklift driver traded me forklifts because mine had the rollovers to dump stuff.

"When I was done, I was driving back into the boiler room. One of the guys was waving me, 'Come on, come on.' By this time my glasses are fogging up. I wasn't seeing too well, but he was telling me, 'Come,' and I was coming. All of a sudden he waves his arms crosswise in front of him. That means it's a washout. Stop immediately. Next thing I know the sky is falling. The forklift had hit the header in the doors and busted it. It all came down on top of me. I was like, 'Oh my gosh, I'm fired,' because I mean I did some damage.

"I backed out and took the forklift to sixth bay. I started walking to my foreman's office to tell him what I had done. All the men were leaning back against the rail with their arms folded. They're like, 'Hey, Crash. How's it going, Crash?' News traveled so fast from one end of the shop to the other! I was so embarrassed. My foreman already knew what I had done, but it was all good. I didn't get fired. He said, 'You learned something, didn't you?' I said, "Yeah. Never trust John Cadillo to give you directions.' It was a good experience.

"I work with a lot of really good people—just normal people like the rest of us out there making a living for their family. Good people.

"I work around hundreds of men every day. They are all so respectful. We'd love to have more women at the railroad. There's only like ten of us in the area that I work. Women can do this job. We have women electricians, women machinists, women firemen/oilers and women foremen. We have women in management. It's a good job. It's a great way to support your family.

"If someone's having trouble—a death in their family, or going through a divorce or having problems with children—any kind of stress that keeps you from being there mentally for your job, you can call Peer Support. I belong to it and I love it because it's being there for someone. That's what life's all about, isn't it?

"I'm a member of Red Block. If you see someone intoxicated or under the influence of drugs, you pull them aside and talk to them to get them to go home so they're not working unsafe around other people.

"You might have to take it a step further and bring it to management's attention which you really don't want to do. It's just being there to help people get through life's bumps.

"Friend-to-Friend is like United Way. Things happen, you have a death in the family or somebody's out of work. Friend to Friend gives money to help pay bills.

"We have the food pantry. If somebody is struggling we make sure they get food baskets while they're out of work.

"There's a lot of positive support. We have a great bunch of people.

"All in all, it's a wonderful job—other than the hours you put in and having to work the holidays. That's the hardest part, not having Christmas with your family. And we can be forced over. Say a few people don't show up to work, you have to stay another four hours. It happens a lot when the weather's bad. That was hard raising kids.

"After I got hired I did push-ups and set-ups every night, trying to get myself strong enough to fuel a locomotive. You have these big fuel lines. They're on a boom. You have to pull them down and then you've got to get them to the locomotive. The fuel spout is up above my head. Being a woman and not having that much upper body strength, I go to pull it and I can't bring it down. So I lift my knees and use my whole body. The next thing you know the boom goes and it's dragging me. I'm holding on to this thing and I'm being dragged

back. It lays me down and then it pulls me back up and then I'm running with this fueler. I'm trying to get it up in that thing and clamped on so I can put the fuel in. I had waffle marks all over the back of my t-shirt. It was the hardest thing. I went home and did push-ups and set-ups to build my strength.

"One night we were having 60 mph winds. The snow was like six inches deep. I come out of the front of a locomotive and the wind took the door. At the same time it took hold of me. I grabbed hold of the rail and here I am, flapping in the wind. It took my hard hat away. I'm hanging on that locomotive and my legs are just flying in the wind. We never did find my hard hat. There are challenges when the weather's bad. I still wouldn't change it. It's a great job. It really is.

"I had five part time jobs before the railroad because I had to support my children. I weighed and measured fish species for Game and Parks, did security at NPPD, was jackie-of-all-trades at the ethanol plant, had my own cleaning business, worked at the church and worked at Parr's I-80. I was all over the place.

"When I got my interview for the railroad I prayed so hard because I'd have one job and know where I was going every day. I plan to finish out my 20 years, Lord willing, and spend time with my grandbabies. I have 12 of them. I'm happy I'll have a good retirement and not have to struggle like a lot of senior citizens."

Mandy Foster

"I was a fireman/oiler from 2003 until 2009. People are all, 'What's a fireman/oiler?' It's generally picking up after people, stocking cabs and cleaning. I stocked the locomotives with ice and water, toiletries, toilet paper, paper towels and hand cleanser. I washed the inside and the outside of the locomotives. We'd have to harness ourselves to the top part of the cab so we could sit and wash the windows. We cleaned the running boards too so nobody would slip and fall on them. Cleaning the toilet wasn't the funnest job in the world. The things that I saw inside the bathroom area... that's what face shields are for.

"We sprayed soap and water on the car bodies and then physically scrubbed around the whole entire car body with a little brush like on a broomstick handle. We would also get up on top of the car. To clean the inside, we opened up all the doors. We sprayed a degreaser on if it was pretty nasty. We had hot water to get the oil off and there are drain holes in the side.

"I drove the locomotive in and out of the shop at times. The only job that I didn't ever do was clean locker rooms. The title Mechanical Service Operator makes a lot more sense than fireman/oiler because we didn't put out fires and we didn't oil anything.

"I fueled the locomotives. Everybody watched me do that because I'm so short. The place where the fuel goes in is above my head. There is a big huge tower with the hose coming off of it. I would hold the fuel nozzle in my arms and go down past where it needed to go in and try to lock it in before the slack went out. If you overfilled it, the fuel would come out another hose which would give you another job to have to clean up.

"Working with men? I wouldn't say it's bad to work with mostly men, but I think they gossip more than most women do. I used to say that it's worse than sitting in a coffee shop with a bunch of old ladies. Being a woman working in male-dominated work wasn't too terrible. I would love to do it again. It was a great job. I think in the whole shop there were maybe ten or fifteen women and we all got along really well. Women are laborers, machinists, electricians, foremen—every aspect of the railroad has women involved in it. The thing I liked best about my job was the friendships that I made.

"The hardest part for me was moving a locomotive. You have to make sure that you're safe and following the rules. You have to make sure that everybody else is out of the way and being safe in their own right. Just the stress of having all that on your mind was hard.

"Safety is talked about every day. We had our morning safety briefing to discuss the rule of the day. The rule book is this big huge book with very small writing. They pick out a rule every day and go over what that rule means. We had training on how to properly get on and off a locomotive. You can't walk and talk to yourself and you can't walk around with your hands in your pockets because you could trip and couldn't catch yourself. There's a rule for everything. There needs to be to keep people safe.

"We wore jeans, steel-toed boots and gloves. One of the guys that I worked with got extra large ones. I got extra small ones which are like these little bitty things. You wore anything that you didn't care if it got dirty because you got very dirty.

"We had a single stall shower in the women's. There was a lunchroom with tables galore that everybody could go in. We had our own refrigerator and microwave. Sometimes I would eat in the locker room because sometimes I just wanted to get away from all the guys. Sometimes us girls would just sit in the locker room and talk.

"You have to be trained on every single aspect of the job. Until you pass, you can't do it by yourself. You have to wear a blue hat for your first year out there. The ones that wear blue hats are the new guys that are in training. After a year you get a yellow hat which means you're qualified on everything and can bid whatever job you want to bid as long as you have the seniority to bid it.

"My husband Cody is in maintenance of way. My dad JK Coleman Sr is an engineer. My little brother Kevin Coleman is a fireman/oiler right now. Also I have uncles and cousins that work for UP as well. The family is in almost all departments. We're a railroading family.

"The benefits are awesome. Retirement, insurance—you don't have to worry about any of that stuff when you have a job out there."

Pamela Tallmage

"I'm a fireman/oiler. I've been with Union Pacific seven years. We do everything. We are the support crew for the rest of the crafts. We wash the locomotives. We service the cabs. We move the locomotives in and out of the shop and around the shop so that they're ready to go on the trains. We stock them.

"If you're not in shape, it can be tough to wash a locomotive. We spray them with soap and we scrub them with a long-handled brush. We don't use a special soap. We use a watered-down soap that's like four percent of something. They had scrubber soap back in the day but it burnt people's skin and it ate the paint off of the locomotives so they went to basically dishwasher soap. You've got high-pressured water. There's no automatic car wash for locomotives—not in our area. You do it by hand. You know it's clean when you're exhausted. You say, 'Just get it out the door. They want it on the train. Let it go!'

"It's a man's world—that's just the way it is. I'm lucky. I'm married to a fabulous man that everyone respects out there, so I don't have to deal with a lot of it. Then again, I'm considered the 'Mom Blob'. That's what I call myself out there. I'm the mom. I mother everyone. That's just what I do.

"A man was working on a locomotive and injured himself. He got his wedding band caught. He ended up with a PI (personal injury). He had to have stitches so they started enforcing the no-ring rule in a strong way. They had pretty much left us alone with our wedding

Pam Tallmage (photo courtesy of Morgan Greenwood)

bands, but not any more. I went two days without my wedding band then I called my son-in-law Bryan Gentry. I asked him to tattoo my wedding band on for me and he did. God bless him. It's a work in progress. He re-inks on a regular basis.

"I started working for the railroad because I got tired of having three husbands and two sons. I was an office manager. I had my husband, I had my boss, and there was another man that worked for them. It was like having three husbands. Another man worked there and of course I have my son. I just started having a nervous breakdown. I said, 'I have to find a different job.' And I chose the railroad. It's like now I have nine hundred. But that's how I got started. I just really was looking for a change. At the railroad there are so many different opportunities you can work into and around that if a job starts driving you crazy, you can always get off it and go somewhere else.

"In the morning we get our lineup. They tell us what we were going to move in and out of the shop. We wash the locomotives so that they meet federal standards going out. They can't have oil on them. We service the cabs and clean the shop, do the garbage, clean the men's bathrooms. As firemen/oilers we are the support crew for the crafts. We do everything.

"What I like best about it is the people I work with. Seriously. Just fabulous people work out there.

"For me, the most challenging part of the job is the weather. I'm the allergy queen. And we move locomotives in and out in the rain and I hate raindrops on my glasses. That makes me crazy.

"You're dragging around heavy equipment, heavy hoses, high pressure air hoses and that type of thing. You have to be aware so that you don't get injured and people around you don't get injured.

"There are so many rules out there that the majority of them you don't even know. The book on the rules is that big. You never know when you're breaking one.

"My husband started out there fifteen years ago. I was a stay-at-home-mom until my son was in first grade, then I got a part time job. He was twelve when I started with the railroad. My husband and I worked different shifts so my son was never home alone. That's why it's hard for a lot of women to go get a job there—because of the children. You're required to work all different shifts. Holidays? Forget it. You're dreaming. You don't get off when you're lower in seniority. I was very fortunate. When I hired on I was at the top of my seniority class so I was able to pick which shift I broke in on. My husband worked first shift. I chose to break in on midnights so we could get our son back and forth to school and he was never alone. Our daughter was in basic training.

"There are not that many women in the crafts because in the crafts you're required to be trained first, and then there's an apprenticeship. Stop and think about doing that when you have young kids at home. Okay, you go get your two-year degree out at the college. That's do-able—women do that everyday. But then you come out to the railroad and you have to do three more years of it in rotating shifts. Think about that for a single parent.

"When I interviewed, they did tell me, 'You're never going to see your kids again.' But seriously, that's very intimidating for most women. For a single female, I couldn't imagine. I was lucky. My husband was out there. I knew I had the support I needed to do different shifts and do what I needed to do."

Firemen/Oilers Job Description

Today the job done by the engine cleaners in the 1940s is titled Mechanical Service Operator. The following information taken from the Union Pacific website in 2011 still describes the work the women were employed to do sixty years ago. The complete listing can be found at: http://www.unionpacific.jobs.

Overview

Think of the Mechanical Service Operator as part of the trains' pit crew. In this entry-level position, you'll help get the locomotives back on the track, keep them clean and fueled, and keep the shop in shape.
Accountabilities:
> Provide locomotives with all necessary materials (drinking water, sand, spare parts, etc.).
> Scrape engine car body and spray engine parts with solvents to remove grease, oil, and/or sludge.
> Clean assigned areas (sweep floors, empty trash, clean parts, and remove residue off of floors)
> Lift and carry 40 pounds (frequently) and up to 86 pounds (rarely-often with assistance); push/pull at a minimum of 50 pounds.
> Safely and effectively operate shop machines and tools such as high-pressure steam cleaning equipment, locomotive cranes, and sand cranes.
> Understand and follow company and industry safety rules, practices, and procedures, wear prescribed safety apparel; take appropriate action when conditions threaten safety of self or coworkers; ensure equipment and work area are in safe operating condition before starting work.

Work Conditions:
> Must wear personal protective equipment such as safety glasses, safety boots, hard hats, and hearing protection.

They will be working:
> Indoors and outdoors, regardless of weather conditions.
> Working forty-hour work weeks that may include variable shifts with overtime and work on rest days, holidays and weekends.

Salary: $14.66 per hour

Just like the men, the women engine cleaners belonged to the Firemen/Oilers Union, a union that began in 1898 when wages averaged seventeen cents an hour for a twelve-hour day, six-day work week of exhausting physical labor. Some unions had difficulty accepting women members but more members, female or not, gave a union stronger bargaining power. Belonging was a benefit for the women too. As one of the men who worked with them at that time said, "Belonging to the union made them more difficult to get rid of after the war." He paused and cleared his throat before he added, "Not that anybody wanted to."

Carmen

Tena Lucas Craghead

"In September 1989 I started to work for Union Pacific Fruit Express as a laborer cleaning UPFE cars. I was there when the pigs used to come through and we used to have to go over and water them. We laborers had to clean out all the food and trash that was left in the cars and wash and disinfect them so they would be clean for the next load. The bulk carrot cars were ok to clean until they sat around for a while and got rotten. It took three times as long to clean them because they were slimy and gross. A car that had meat scattered throughout was full of maggots and I couldn't eat rice for a long time after that one. The rotten potatoes left in the cars would get maggots as well. To clean the floor, you had to lift up the floor racks with a special bar that the laborers made.

Dorothy Savory, Tena Craghead (photo courtesy of Christy Callendar)

"I worked a year before getting set up as a toolman, which is apprentice carman. I finally got to use my electrical and HVAC (Heating Ventilation and Air Conditioning) degrees. I had to work 733 days as a toolman before I got my carman's date. At that time carmen serviced the refrigerated units and the diesel 271 engines.

"I transferred to UPFE in Pocatello in March 1992. I got laid off in April, got hired by UP in Pocatello, and transferred back to North Platte in May to work for UP in the car department. Carmen have to be certified welders. You got to go to school for air brakes so you're certified for air tests. They've got all kinds of training now.

"I was set up to a foreman in 2000. Now I supervise in east origin yard.

"I've always been a woman in a man's world more or less. I came to college out here in '82 and I was the only woman in all my classes at Voc Tech. I was the first woman working in North Platte on the mechanical side at PFE. When I started in the car department there was only one other gal working as a carmen. Now there are twelve women working in the car department.

"I'm going on twenty-two years now, three years in PFE and all the rest in the car department. I plan to retire in 13 more years. It's the best job I ever had."

Linda May Miller

"I started with the railroad about five years ago. I'm a carman.

"We make sure the brakes on the cars work right. We do air tests. One person sits up in the unit (the locomotive) and sets the brakes and releases them. Two guys in-truck run one on each side of the train. They make sure all the pistons come out—that the cars set up so that the brakes will stop the car when the engineer sets the brakes. If it doesn't pass the test, we have another carman that comes and does the air repair. They make the repair and do another air test to make sure it sets and releases and it's on its way. It usually takes about half an hour to do an air test on a hundred-car train. That's if everything goes good. If they can't fix them then they have to set that car out.

"We fix the wheels right inside the train now instead of having to pull them out. The new system uses a jack called a pump truck. I ran it for a while. You leave the train together and it goes in between the couplers where the cars hook together. It lifts the car straight up in the air about four or five feet. Another machine comes

in and grabs the wheel and pulls it off. We grab a new one off the truck and slip it right back in there. Then we put the jack down. It takes longer to lock up the train than it does to change the wheel. It takes ten minutes to change the wheel and about fifteen to twenty minutes to lock up the train, but most of the trains will have two or three wheels to fix.

"They usually hire three or six in a group. When I got hired I was the only one in my group. You sit in the classroom for six weeks then they put you out in the yards. You always hear the old guys talking, 'Well, when I hired on, you got the job and the next day you're out there in the yard doin' work.' They don't do that any more. They walk you through everything and show you how to do it so hopefully nobody gets hurt. You learn a lot in class but you learn a lot more working at the yards.

"We change brake shoes. We'll be standing in there changing a shoe on coal one and coal two will start rolling in. You'll hear the unit, but the cars are so quiet you hardly hear them. And you have earplugs in. If you aren't paying attention, you'll just walk right into it.

"I work midnights—eleven to seven. I went to midnights so I could spend the evenings with the kids and be able to pick them up after school. They've been really good about me working. They don't quite understand the 'you need to let mom sleep,' but they've done real well. They think the big trains are cool. They want to go see them up close.

"They just had layoffs. That's the first time they've laid off since the eighties, but they've brought everybody back and they've rehired.

"The car department is one of the better places to be. I've had transportation say the carmen seem to have a little better deal. We don't have to go out on the road. I have a set schedule. We get called for overtime, but that's your choice. Holidays, we don't have to work.

"I work in the east run-thru. It's the fueling racks. I'm light repair so if they have problems with a hand brake or something that we can fix quick, then we go. We'll cut the brake or set the car out, stuff like that. We make sure there's nothing dragging; make sure that there's nothing major. If we can't fix it then we set the car out. Otherwise, all I do is shoe. We look at the brake shoes and make sure they're thick enough. Every once in a while you'll get one that's burnt in and basically it's the metal to the metal. You have to cut them out with a torch. That's my job. I like cutting stuff up. I'm not very good fixing it, but I can cut it up."

"We have a rip where there's three tracks. That's where they do most of the big repairs, anything we can't do in the yards. They have the heavy jacks and everything in there.

"Everyday you run into something you've never seen before; you learn something. The old guys will tell you that too.

"Ninety-some percent of the bums that are on the trains have warrants out for their arrest. I usually just lock the truck door and call them in. Basically the only thing I have that would protect me would be a shoeing bar. That's a three-foot crowbar, but good luck swinging that. I'd rather just lock my truck doors.

"I worked in the departure yard where they build the trains. They bring cars up over the hump and build the trains. We walked them and buckled them—that's hooking the air hoses together.

"It takes you fifteen minutes to get dressed—hard hat, glasses, earplugs, steel-toed shoes, and now our new thing is we have a yellow vest that has reflector tape on it that we have to wear all the time. When we get out of our truck we have to have it all on except for the earplugs. The only time we have to have our earplugs on is when we're 150 feet away from a unit because they're so loud. Either that or welding or using the torch, so you don't get anything in your ears.

"We put FREDs on—those are the little boxes you see blinking on the back when there's not a unit back there. If they need to dump the train (lock the brakes) that little box on the back that blinks will dump it from the rear, so the rear cars lock up. They can also dump it from the head end and it will meet in the middle and stop a lot faster. They'll still travel a mile. It depends on how much weight's behind them. They'll come in and have cow hair or deer hair on the front of the locomotive. They cannot stop. It's gross. But you know, between a twelve hundred pound bull and a unit that weighs a hundred tons and has loaded coal cars behind it... there's just no way.

"I've had good experiences. I haven't had any problems. I think the guys expect more out of you because you are a woman so when you do your job you gotta do it better than they do. The people I work with are good people. Everybody seems to take care of each other. If it looks like somebody's going to get hurt, they're right there telling you, 'No, I wouldn't do that.'

"I plan on staying out there as long as I can. I plan on retiring out there. It's a good job."

Dorothy Savory (photo courtesy of Morgan Greenwood)

Dorothy Keck Savory

"I am a fifth generation railroader down from my great-great-grandfather to myself. My dad and brothers all worked the railroad. It's always been an important part of our life. Always. With my dad that's all I can ever remember. We owned a costume shop in Grand Island, but we had the hugest train set you've ever seen in the basement when we were kids.

"I work at Bailey Yard in the car department. I started in November 1998. There are approximately 320 carmen in our department. Approximately 10 are women.

"I, as a single parent, decided I needed a better job. I was broke always. The insurance alone is worth it to me—you just can't beat it.

"Working for the railroad among that many men is great. I can't say I have a problem whatsoever. I get treated equally which I really do like. If you have something to say, you say it. If they have something to say, they say it. You just accept it. I grew up with seven brothers and two sisters, a pretty tight-knit family, so I have no problem being around men. Or women. It's a great place to be.

"Our job is fascinating but I don't think people understand what we do. They see us in trucks. They think we just run up and down a train. There is so much more to our job. We are inspecting every aspect of that car from the beginning to the end starting with a coupler. You have to inspect probably 49 car components if not more, and that's just on the car body. When you inspect the air, you're looking at another 49 plus. Inspection to me is really important—not just because there are other people out there. My brothers are on those trains. They're conductors. I want to make sure that everybody is safe. That's another issue out there, the safety issue. You really really want to make sure you're going home and the people you're working with are going home. You've got to be alert.

"I guess I would have to say as a female it's an amazing job. One I never thought I would ever do. I didn't realize how much detail there is in the learning. I've been out there 13 years and I am still learning. There's something new all the time. It's just extremely fascinating. I think it's great that we have women in the department—women not afraid to do the work and not afraid to ask questions.

"Besides working the trains, I work in the tower. There are about eight tower-qualified people. That's a totally other job in the car department. We keep the times that people are on the trains and off the train. We're dealing with Omaha; we're dealing with other towns; we're dealing with bad orders. A bad order means it's something that absolutely cannot be repaired in train and it's got to go to our shop (which is called the rip) and it gets repaired there. That's heavy repair.

"Carmen are light repair people. There are lots of repair you can do. It just depends on what it is, whether it be an air problem, service portion or emergency portion. It's amazing. I wish you could see a shoe so you would know what I mean when I say changing a shoe.

"We also have a road truck. Guys go out in a very large road truck and make repairs. They're still regular carmen but they called to go out if there's a derailment whether it be in the yards or out anywhere in the road.

"It's so overwhelming when you first get hired on. My first year I remember calling in to my foreman and asking him to come take a look at this whachama-callit.

"He came back over the radio and said, 'What did you call it?'

"I said, 'A whachamacallit. I don't know what this is, but it doesn't look right.'

"'Ok. I'll be out to check out that whachamacal-lit.'

"To this day people who were working that night will say to me, 'Hey, you got any whachamacallits that need looked at?'

"Trains are dangerous. As a little girl I rode on a passenger train from Grand Island to Oregon. You don't think about it. You see a train and it's a train. It's going by. People do need to be aware of the fact that trains are dangerous. They're not a toy to be hopping on.

"Another scary thing is when you've got somebody who's riding a train in the middle of the night. You're not aware that they're there, but you find out real fast, let me tell you. I don't want to get out of my truck for a couple of nights after that.

"You got to have fun. Everything can't be all work. It's supposed to be but you got to laugh. You got to joke, even if it's blowing off steam in a fun way. You get to be really good friends with a lot of people. As in every workplace you have some that you might not care for, but you're working with them—so work with them. Just because you're not going to hang out and be best buds, that doesn't matter. You want to make sure they're safe and that everybody's going home to their family—that's the most important thing.

"I'm a single parent: three kids, 30, 28 and 19. I've been a single parent since the oldest were 2 and 3. When it came up that they were hiring, I knew I had to take a chance at it. I wasn't sure if I would like it or not, but I needed to support my kids and keep them going.

"It's pretty fascinating. I'm only 51 and I've got a ways to go before I can retire. I plan on staying healthy and fit and not getting hurt so I'm going to be out there a long time. I know people retire and it's kind of sad—don't get me wrong—you want people to retire because that's a seniority move for you. At the same time when they're gone, it's a big void. You do miss hearing that person or you do miss hearing their joke or you might miss their grumpiness because it's part of you out there. You're family out there. I'm not going to speak on everybody's behalf but I personally think we're family. Second family.

"Our job is so important. I know they make jokes, "Oh, the carmen don't do anything.' Or the carmen do this, or carmen do that. They don't understand that we know what we're looking for.

"I have my own way to inspect a train. Starting from the end I know what I'm looking for everywhere. My eyes are up and down. Everybody's got their own way to inspect. What they don't understand is that we are out there inspecting those trains to make sure that a car is not getting out of town that could involve a derailment or a crew having a problem.

"I like my job. I love my job actually. There are days I don't want to go to work when it's really nasty outside and stuff. But I'm there.

"The work that I do makes a tremendous impact on the world because of the different kinds of cars that you deal with. Most important would be a loaded stacker. That is known as a hot pot item. You've probably seen them. There'll be 3-packs or 5-packs. They're containers stacked on top of each other. It's called an intermodal car. There's a huge variance in what they carry. Those are hot. Those got to get from here to there. It could be your mail. It could be your canned goods. You've got your auto racks carrying cars. Then you've got the coal. East run-thru we've got coal that runs through there like crazy. Our job is all about that. We are getting that train inspected so it can be out of town.

"Does anybody like a bad order? No, because that means that car has to be set out. That's going to affect the shipper; it's going to affect us; it affects the people out there in the world that it's getting shipped to. That's the reason, if you can fix the car within the train, it needs fixed within the train. If they're empty it's not a huge impact. The loaded ones you want to be sure you do what you can to get that moving. Our job is huge as far as how we affect everybody anywhere. It's huge. Huge."

Clerks

Diana Hitchcock

"I'm a utility clerk. I started about four years ago. I saw the job on the internet. My sister told me, 'You could do that. You're good at driving and bossing people around.'

"Utility clerks do different things. The driving is probably the main, but there are also the janitors. One goes to the outside buildings; the inside janitor cleans the yard office.

"There's probably four men in our area at the yard office. The rest are women. I believe there's twenty-six of us including janitors and the YOS (yard office supervisors). There are three shifts. The day shift has three janitors, the yard supervisor, and three to four drivers. Just for fun in the yard, I tell the daylighters that the night people are the most efficient, that we get the most done. The old heads are mostly on the day shift so that statement gets them a little fired up.

"We have to know how to get around to all the different crossings and which ones we can go on and which ones to stay away from. We always say that we could drive sixty miles and end up back where we started. Really it's just one big circle. The farthest away we normally go is to the west run-thru. That takes roughly eleven minutes. The shortest is probably to the shop. On a good run you can make that in two. It just depends on how many carmen or fuel truck drivers are in the way.

"We might have to go across a different crossing to get the crew closer to the engine because they don't like to walk. Some of their luggage—they call them grips— has to be at least a hundred pounds because of the stuff they're required to carry: log-in books, all the rules and everything—a lot of stuff. And then they bring their meals, so some of them have, oh, three or four bags, plus a cooler. We don't carry them. They try to trick the newbies, but we warn them ahead of time.

"The YOS are the ones that tell us which track to go to to pick up the crew, or which crew needs to go to a certain track. They'll tell us and we'll try to get them there within a reasonable amount of time. It depends on how much is blocking our way. The YOS get on the computer. They know which trains are pulling out and where we might be blocked at a crossing, or if they're setting out a bad order. If it's one of the long trains it's going to block two or three crossings, so we might have to go around. Or we can sit and wait.

"The crew is the engineer and the conductor, sometimes a brakeman, sometimes a trainee. Sometimes a manager might be with them. Usually you can spot them. They're a little more clean. They're the ones with a little fancier clothes. They just don't look like a normal person I guess.

"They're making the trains really, really long now. Some trains are too big to go on certain rails so they have to cut them apart. When they want to leave town they have to put them back together. When they're putting them back together, they shoot across the whole yard, then they have to back in, so there are four or five crossings they can block. Every once in a while something will break down and they might sit there for a couple of hours. If a rail breaks, you know they won't be leaving town. If they're fixing rails, we're told to stay out of the area as much as possible.

"We do have to wear special things. We have the glasses, the earplugs and steel-toes boots. If we're out of the van in a red zone—which is so many feet from the power—we wear a vest.

"I work nights, which is my preferred shift. I'm one of the older clerks out there but I'm still one of the babies. I was the baby for three years before they hired anybody else. It's a good job with good benefits. It doesn't really stress you out too much. Some of the guys are kind of amusing. They'll give each other a little bit of ribbing. Some of them when they get off the trains, they're a little crabby because they might have had to wait a half hour or so. The number of drivers we have just isn't enough to pick everybody up, especially if we're real busy.

"A lot of them know our names because there's so few of us. I don't know very many of theirs because there are so many and it's dark. When I work, I just tell them that they all look alike and they smell the same, so I'm sorry I can't tell you apart. That usually gets them to laugh and breaks the ice a little bit too. I don't like riding with crabby people. It drives me nuts. They give me a lot of guff, too. Some of them we have to remind to hook their safety belt. I tell them, 'Apparently you haven't heard about my driving. I've scared a few rabbits out here.'

"I forgot about dodging rabbits. The rabbits out there are huge. There are quite a few of them, but the strange thing is you never see a baby and you very rarely see a dead one. They are fast and smart. They're about knee high. Biggest jackrabbits I've ever seen in my life. And there is a little herd of deer everybody gets a kick out of watching. They have their babies out there, and they aren't scared of anything. Those trains are around them all the time. They'll go under them and it's amazing the limbo that they do, how low to the ground they get—just like a dog.

"They have names for the different places. The lady engineers and the lady conductors, when their train isn't ready at east run-thru, they wait in this little building called the Bull Pen. I always thought that was funny. They should change that. There's a sign on it too that says 'Bull Pen'.

"The worst out there is when it's foggy and snowy. Last year we got like eight inches in an hour. They weren't able to get it cleared off. We didn't know where the crossings were. You couldn't see them. One thing they tell us is, 'Follow the carmen. They know where to go.' Not true. I got stuck on the rail. It looked like a crossing. The carmen got across. They know how to ramp their trucks. You call the yard office. They'll call whoever they need to and say, 'OK, we've got someone stuck. Don't send anything down that track.' I've been able to get myself off most of them. It's just that shock. You don't want to panic whatever you do because it will just make things worse.

"It's amazing how quiet the cars can roll on the tracks. You think something that big you're going to hear, but you don't always.

"Once in a while we get called in for overtime. We can say yes or no. It's good money, but you know, you need a life too. Family's tough out there. You gotta know your priorities. I hated afternoons. I was on them for a while, but it always seemed like I couldn't get anything done. In the mornings, you had to get ready for work and couldn't start any projects, and by the time you got home it was 11:00. What do you do at 11:00 P.M.? Go to bed. So I like nights. I can do whatever I want to during the day and then go to work at night. It works out great."

Crafts

Rose Roth

Rose Roth has been with UPRR since 1991. She hired on as a fireman/oiler in the mechanical department. She completed a three-year electrical apprenticeship and has worked as an electrician and as a foreman at the shop, service track, and coal trains. She worked with the DPU (Distributed Power Locomotive) team as an electrician and peer trainer. Rose is currently an electrician at the diesel shop.

Rose likes her job and she says, "If you are a tomboy and not afraid to get dirty, it's a career to consider." Rose's daughter Stacey Tansey works in the transportation department. Rose says, "Working for the same company helps us understand each other's work experiences."

Rose Roth and her daughter Stacey Tansey

Maegan Peterson

"I have been at the railroad for five and a half years. I started out as a fireman/oiler cleaning engines, moving units in and out of the shop, and making up sets for the trains.

"When firemen/oilers clean a car body, they hand-scrub the entire top half of the unit—basically all of the yellow—to make it look better. It takes anywhere from two and a half to three hours depending on how dirty it is, how clean you can get it, or how clean they need it. You scrub with just a normal brush on a handle. It's a lot of hard work.

"They have 'specials' for units that are going for calendar pictures or to pull the CEO or the president. With Rail Fest coming up, we'll have units that need specials—a top-to-bottom cleaning. We'll scrub the paint, the handrails, the trucks, the snowplows, the front and back—it all has to be as spotless as it can be.

"I decided to go for foreman because I wanted a little more responsibility. I've been fix-it foreman, a reliability foreman and now I'm second-shift outbound foreman.

"Fix-it fixes anything broken that comes in. Reliability is road failures that come in—the really, really broken stuff that needs a little more time to troubleshoot. Second-shift outbound is responsible for the stuff that's built for the trains. We do air tests, electricians' tests and check all the CCS safety equipment.

"As foreman I make sure everyone has their reports signed off and everyone is safely doing their job. There are a couple of different titles that we go by—foreman, mechanical supervisor, or locomotive supervisor.

"After I graduated college I came back to work in the assessor's office in the courthouse. I'm diabetic. I missed my dad's insurance so I decided to go get my own through the railroad. The benefits and the pay are just outstanding.

"Working in a man's environment is definitely a lot different than working around an office full of females. You have to talk to guys in a different way. You have to have tough skin when you're out there. You gotta learn to joke around with them because if you don't, they'll pick on you more. You gotta be able to hold your own weight. You know, if one of the guys picks on you, be able to fire something back at him. You have to do your work to your fullest ability. The guys know that I worked my tail end off as a fireman/oiler. They heard from other people that I was a good worker. Your work ethic doesn't go unnoticed out there.

"The most challenging part of my job is finding that fine line between your managers and your workers. You, being in the middle, have to know what to pass on from the managers or to the managers, and how to stick up for your guys. And I have to trust them to do their job.

"At first what I liked best was the fact that I didn't have to get up an hour early to get dressed for work.

"At one time I wanted to become a manager and took the management test, but I like where I am right now. I like the responsibility that I have as a supervisor. I pretty much like all the people that work out there. Everyone makes you laugh and we all have a good time, but we still get our work done.

"On a typical day I make up a track list for the hostlers so they can move their units. I get a turnover from the tower and basically get prepped for my shift. I learn what's left over from the previous shift. I look up the units, transfer them to the computer, and line the guys up. We do our safety talk in the morning. It's our SQP (Safety, Quality, and Production). Our sheet has our rule of the day and any safety incidents that happened across the system that we need to be aware of. I address the guys' concerns and make sure everything's signed. I relay all that stuff on to the manager in charge. It's a lot of computer work.

"During foreman training you go to each job for a week and break in with a supervisor. Basically that's all it is—hands-on. Your first one or two days, you watch that foreman. They explain what's going on. The third day

Maegan Peterson (photo courtesy of Morgan Greenwood)

they let you do some of that job. By the fourth and fifth day you're doing it by yourself. The foreman is there if you need any help or have any questions. They're there, but you are doing that job. Basically you get thrown in and you have to pick it all up.

"After you're a foreman, you go to supervising degree classes. I believe there are four of them. The first one is a week long about communication, then conflict management, then presentations, and then you go to your final, which I have not been to yet. Every foreman gets that training.

"I am union, not management. The managers are the non-agreement. I'm in the mechanical department. It consists of electricians, machinists, pipefitters and boilermakers. Our area consists of the diesel shop, the service track, outbounds and reliability. G.E. has their side in the shop and at the service track. Also we have the east coal train rack. They run trains through those to be serviced. Then we have our west coal.

"I would tell any woman that wanted to work on the railroad to be prepared, have tough skin. It is a hard and dirty job, but it's well worth it. If you have a good work ethic, it's a great job. You will probably have to work every shift, so be prepared for that. It's hard to be away from your family and your little ones on midnights and second shift. On daylights you're a little more normal than what you are on second and third shifts.

"My dad has worked out there for thirty-nine and a half years. My grandfather retired from there. I am a third generation railroader. My mom laughs because my dad and I will be 'talking railroad' and she doesn't quite understand it. I have one little three-year-old boy who is infatuated with trains. Any shows on tv with trains he enjoys. He likes to go out and drive past the trains. I've taken him into the diesel shop a couple of times. He just is in awe of it all. He's talking about how he wants to drive a train one day."

Medical

Misti M. Brown

"I got started with Union Pacific Railroad through a co-worker who convinced me to apply. This has been a positve move for me. Union Pacific is a great company with great benefits and great professional opportunities.

"Being a nurse out here is really not different from being a nurse anywhere else. It's just a different setting. The nurses are here to address illnesses and injuries, do

health screenings and also to facilitate and educate the employees about healthy lifestyle choices. UP has a wealth of programs to assist employees to pursue healthy life choices so they can live healthy and enjoy a healthy retirement.

"Every month there are different topics—topics like heat stress, diabetes and healthy eating habits—that we present to the employees. We also teach CPR classes that include how to use an AED (defribullator). AEDs are available in many of the work locations. With the CPR/AED training we want people to know how to initiate CPR and use it if they have to. It is important piece of the education that the nurses prepare employees and supervisors to respond to cardiac situations in the workplace.

"We approach employees at lineups at the beginning of their shifts when they get their job assignment. Building relationships and gaining employees' trust is a must. The employees are receptive and many times come over to the office for a one on one discussion to talk about health issues or just visit about what is going on in their lives. I think that's great. It's the only way you can get to know the employee as an individual and gain insight into how we can assist them.

"Union Pacific has a Chief Medical Office that is based out of Omaha that oversees the Occupational Nurse program and writes the Clinical Protocols and Directives. We also have a local practicing physician here in North Platte who assists with our vaccines such as tetanus and flu. The nurses have clinical protocols to follow for their nursing practice at UPRR. We respond

Misti Brown (photo courtesy of Morgan Greenwood)

to illness and injury and follow up with the employee on an individual basis. We use training, experience and the clinical protocols to guide us in our response. The goal is to prevent injury and illness before it happens and maintain safety for everyone. Safety is essential in the workplace and the nurses are part of that Total Safety Culture on the railroad. We even have out own personal protective equipment, (PPE) so we can respond in the field to emergencies and to talk with employees in the field.

"There are five nurses for North Platte, three for the service unit and two for the diesel shop. Among the five nurses, we cover call 24/7. We work together and cover a large area. I recently went to Kearney, Lexington and Fairbury and on the way back, stopped in Hastings. We've got another nurse out today traveling to Bridgeport and South Morrill. These site visits allow for education, health counseling, health screening, AEDs and distributing new health information to the employees. We also do health screenings such as blood pressure checks, cholesterol and blood glucose screens, respiratory fit testing and body mass index evaluations. We review the results with the employee and go over any target areas that the individual may need to focus on. It's a helpful tool to get people focused and informed about issues with their individual health.

"My decision to join the UP family was a positive move, not only for myself, but also for my family. The flexibility and support from UP is key. UP supports continuing education, professionalism and professional growth and as a nurse that weighs heavily. Continued education and training is also a part of the Occupational Health Program and it is so important to keep technically current in our nursing career."

Sammy Hansen

"I have been employed for the Union Pacific Railroad for 12 years as occupational health nurse. We are under Health and Medical in the Human Resource Department in Omaha. My job entails a lot of interaction with people. If someone is injured we take care of their injury and refer them to the doctor or hospital if they need to go. We provide emergency care, depending on the extent of the injury. We do a lot of health promotion and health teaching. We encourage people to exercise and eat right. We have quality safety meetings on cholesterol, the benefits of exercise and eating healthy. In the summer we educate people how to prevent heat stroke and heat exhaustion.

Sammy Hansen (photo courtesy of Morgan Greenwood)

"We go to the lineups and provide education. Where they work, it's 24/7 so we're out there around the clock doing educational presentations. We're working on a new program. Employees sign up for six sessions with a professional trainer who designs an exercise program for them. I think we have a hundred and thirty-four in our program. The railroad pays for them to go to an exercise facility.

"We have fitness meals once a month. At those meals we have a speaker, usually a medical professional who teaches them about health and taking care of themselves. We encourage employees to see their physician and be checked out when they reach 50. Of course we have the scales and body fat measurement, and BMI—boys like toys, so they come in and talk to us. They weigh and check their body fat and have their cholesterol checked.

"We check for blood sugar, and A1C's, which gives you a total of what your blood sugar has been over the past three months. We have all those machines out there. We draw their blood and give them instant results. We take lots of blood pressures.

"Once a year we have our health fair. Vendors come from town. Last year we had a podiatrist, a cardiologist and an urologist. We always try to do a nutritionist. Someone from the hospital does diabetic teaching. We have counselors on site for stress and counseling in a private area. We have the fun things, like massage therapists. They have had a good day by the time we get done. Of course we have food and drinks and prizes. We enjoy doing it, and they look forward to having it. We draw their blood a month before and do a venous sample that is sent to the hospital and analyzed. A copy is sent to their own personal physician. We give them a copy and explain their blood work to them. If there's any critical marker, they're sent to their physician right away.

"I got started at the Union Pacific because of Dr. Brittan. He provided nurses by contract. After several years the railroad decided to hire nurses. We have been UP employees for about the last three years.

"It's fun working in a man's environment. I've always said give me ten thousand men to work with rather than one woman. It's a good environment for us as nurses. We're well respected. Trust and respect is what it's all about. They have to trust and respect the nurse before they'll confide in us and tell us their concerns.

"The greatest challenge is getting people interested in preventive health care. Men like to wait until they have symptoms. Women are much easier to convince that they need to practice preventive health. Men are much harder because, you know, they're strong. There's nothing wrong with them until there's something really wrong with them.

"The best part of my job is the interaction with the people. I'm a people person. I have a four-year degree in nursing but my higher learning has occurred out there. I have heard a lot of stories and intriguing things about the old roundhouse and how they used to do things, and how the safety has improved through the years.

"We get quite a few night calls. Normally we work eight to five. There's a nurse that works on the evening shift until about 11. A nurse comes in about five in the morning.

"We do all the regulatory testing. That is another big job because of OSHA. They have to have a hearing test every year. There's like nine hundred people just in the shop that we're responsible testing their hearing. If they work on the sand crane they have to wear respirator masks. There are about four hundred people that have to be respirator fit tested. We don't do anything with the drug testing. We're the friendly nurses. We don't want to get involved in that.

"We probably have 34 nurses system-wide. In North Platte there are five: two at the superintendent's office in the car department, one nurse at the run-thru, and two nurses at the diesel shop.

"All of our interaction is HIPAA-protected, and confidential just like the doctor's office and the hospital. If something is reported to us, we can't report it to anyone. It's up to the person to report an injury. We can't report it.

"We go out in the yards and in the shop. We have our AEDs (automatic external defibrillators) for heart attacks. Those are all around the shop and in the outlying service track areas. We check those. We maintain the first aid kits and first aid cabinets. We do a walkaround in the shop and interact with the employees. We observe them for good body mechanics and remind them to do their stretching exercises. If we see somebody working in a really bad position, we stop and remind them that they need to get out of that position and stretch and relax just a little bit, hoping that we prevent back strains and knee strains and sprains.

"Every lineup, they do their stretches. It's really a good thing. It prevents a lot of injuries. One person leads them and the rest of them follow.

"I went to the LEAD Conference last summer. It was wonderful. LEAD helps us as women to be leaders. It gives us confidence and helps us to feel our own self-worth. Women make a difference in people's lives."

History of the Union Pacific Fruit Express

Reefers—refrigerated boxcars that are insulated to keep cargo at a regulated temperature—were first used to ship butter in 1851. The original reefer was a wooden boxcar 36 foot long with bunkers along the sides. The bunkers were filled with ice through roof hatches.

In 1857 ice-cooled railcars were introduced to the meat-packing industry in Chicago. These reefers eliminated the need for long cattle drives.

In 1865 Parker Earle, a fruit grower in Illinois, pioneered iced transit for produce. He harvested blocks of ice and packed them in his barn in sawdust. In the spring he filled one side of a large wooden chest with ice and packed the other side with strawberries. He shipped the chests by rail to Chicago where they arrived in perfect condition and sold for as much as $1 a quart.

In 1877 breweries added one and one-half feet of height and five feet of length to make insulated boxcars that could keep a load cool from coast to coast.

In 1889 New York received its first carload of deciduous fruit from California thanks to reefers.

In 1907 Edward H. Harriman created Pacific Fruit Express as a joint venture of the Union Pacific and Southern Pacific. It began operation with a fleet of 6,600 refrigerator cars. PFE's goal was to speed transportation of perishable fruits and vegetables across the country. Maury Klein, in his book *Union Pacific: The Rebirth* states that in 1927 PFE's North Platte plant could provide ice for up to 1000 cars per day. Icing typically took about a minute. Blocks weighing several tons were loaded into hatches at either end of the car while melted icewater was drained off. The melted ice water from the ice house in North Platte was piped about a quarter mile underground to fill the Gerle swimming pool which was east of the where the Buffalo viaduct is now. Frances Johnson and Kris Krzycki used to swim there in the 1940s for ten cents a day. Both agreed it was always cold.

PFE's reefers were painted a Standard Refrigerator yellow color until 1929 when the color was replaced with Standard Refrigerator orange, a yellow-orange color. That color was also discontinued and Union Pacific's reefer cars are now white.

Steel reefers replaced wooden ones in the 1940s but roof hatches were still used to fill the area between the exterior wall and the load with fresh ice about every 400 miles, a process called "stage icing".

The plug door was introduced experimentally by PFE in 1947. Sliding plug doors with hinged extensions provided a six foot opening that facilitated car loading and unloading by making it possible to use fork-lifts. The tight-fitting doors were better insulated and could maintain a more even temperature inside the car.

By 1958 reefers were cooled using diesel powered refrigerator units and mechanical refrigeration began to replace ice-based systems. By the mid-1970s the few remaining ice bunker cars were relegated to "top-ice" service, where crushed ice was applied atop the commodity.

PFE was dissolved in March 1978. Southern Pacific retained the Pacific Fruit Express name. Union Pacific named its half Union Pacific Fruit Express.

In 1984 a $915,000 North Platte complex for cleaning of mechanical refrigerated cars was constructed.

According to an article in the North Platte Telegraph in January, 2000: Priority intermodal trains (trailers and containers on flatcars), called Z trains, depart from Chicago for Los Angeles and Oakland at 70 miles per hour, stopping at NP just long enough for inspection and servicing and to pick up new crews. Similar trains meet ships at the ports of Los Angeles and Long Beach and speed Asian goods to the Midwest and East, after a stop at Bailey.

The Union Pacific Corporation 2009 Analyst Fact Book states: Union Pacific now owns and operates the largest refrigerated boxcar fleet in the industry. Produce Railexpress and Express Lane are UP's premium perishables service offerings. Produce Railexpress carries fresh produce from the West Coast to New York. Express Lane moves dairy products, canned goods, wine, frozen foods and some fresh produce from the West Coast to destinations in the East and Southeast. California and Washington, the states directly served by these products, provide over 60 percent of the nation's fresh fruits and vegetables. Additionally, the Railroad transports frozen

North Platte Ice House (torn down in 1973) (photo courtesy of Kaycee Anderson)

meat and poultry from the Midwest and Mid-South to the West Coast for export.

Pacific Fruit Express (PFE)

Eva Melius

"I moved here from South Dakota. I am married and have two girls, 19 and 17. I have a medical transcription degree. I applied at the hospital but they weren't needing anybody.

"I applied to Union Pacific online. I went for an interview and didn't think I had a chance of getting hired, but next day they called and wanted to hire me. I've been doing it for six years now and have learned a lot.

"My job title is carman but basically I'm a fuel truck driver. I fill up the reefer cars with diesel. I pump between 5000 and 6000 gallons of fuel a night depending on how many cars we get in the yard. Each car is a refrigeration unit run by diesel and each one holds 500 gallons of fuel. The other night we had 48 come in. It took me an hour and a half to fuel them. How long it takes depends on how empty they are and how many cars are on the train.

"The cars come from all over. We've got two trains, one from California and one from Washington. They have nothing but reefer cars on them. They're called the Z trains. They go from the west coast to the east coast in a week. Usually they're fueled in Washington and we don't have to fuel them here unless they're really low on fuel. We read the fuel gauges, but we also have people in Omaha who monitor them by satellite. They'll say, 'Hey, catch this train when it stops, put fuel in such and such car because it's running low and might die.'

"They can tell what temperature the car is supposed to be set at and if it's set in that range. If it dies, they can tell what it died from—engine stall, battery voltage, door open etc. Sometimes it just dies or doesn't want to start because it's so cold. Maybe the fuel's gelled up.

"When the train arrives we flag it out which means we put blue flashing lights and locks on both ends so that train does not move because we've got people climbing on and off that train.

"The Z trains usually come into the new coal yard. They're high priority trains and they don't stay very long, maybe an hour and a half at the most. They change crews and they change engines and they're gone. They usually average 50 to 80 cars on the train.

"In the summer if we have a lot of cars come in that can't be repaired right away, or if the temperatures get

Eva Melius (photo courtesy of Morgan Greenwood)

way too high, we lose the load. It happens. It's mechanical; it's gonna break. UP will call the company to see if they want to donate it to a food pantry if it's a loss, but salvageable. Other than that it's goes in the dump.

"We get loads of potatoes, peaches, apples, onions, strawberries, tomato paste, cheese, wine—you name it. If it needs to be refrigerated to be shipped, we ship it.

"We work in all kinds of weather—rain, snow, sleet, and sweltering heat.

"I trained for a week. It doesn't take too much training. If you can squeeze a fuel nozzle or climb a ladder you're good to go. They showed me how to run a fuel truck and a week later they turned me loose because we were short on manpower. I was scared to death. I didn't know where I was going or what I was doing but I told myself, *Ok, I can do this.* I did get a lot of safety training and watched a lot of safety films. We update our training annually to make sure we're up to speed.

"My husband thinks it's great I work for the railroad. My kids? It's just another job Mom has to do. But they think it's neat. When we first moved here, they liked going around the trains and seeing the yard. They were just amazed at how big the yard is. It's the biggest in the world. It's huge. I didn't realize how big until I drove it. It's like it never ends.

"When I first hired on I was a fuel truck driver then I started working in the office monitoring the cars. If they were broken or shut down, I'd call to have somebody fix them or check them. Then they moved the office jobs to Omaha. I didn't want to move to Omaha so they put me back driving the fuel truck.

"It does gets monotonous after a while, but we have enough fun. I enjoy it. The worst thing about my job is working in the weather. I work nights so when it gets cold, you're cold. I'm not your wimpy woman. I don't cry and whine and snivel, but the weather is the worst part. Other than that it isn't a bad job.

"Every once in a while you might get a diesel bath. There are two vents on each side of the car. If they're plugged with dirt, oil or whatever, it pressurizes the tank. You go to pull the nozzle out of the tank and it sprays back on you—and you get a diesel bath. And that's no fun. We have a shower at the office and I have a change of clothes in my locker. Most of us do. We just change and continue on. We got a washing machine there. We throw all the clothes in there and wash them. We put those cars on a lookout list and when they go to a cleaning track, they take them apart and clean them and fix what is wrong.

"We have to wear protective gear: steel toed boots, safety glasses, reflective vests, and earplugs. We have to wear earplugs all the time. You get used to it. I feel naked without mine now. I go outside and ftt, they're in. I don't even notice them. I can have a conversation. They don't block out all the noise. They just muffle it so the loud noises don't damage your ears.

"We have three main lines going through the yard right now on the express lane. ARMN—those are our cars. They're white with black letters. The yellow cars—they don't use them anymore. We also monitor TILX, CRYX, and PBRX cars. Those are all reefer cars owned by other companies. If they want us to repair or fuel them, they send us a fax.

"I'm ex-military so railroad's nothing for me. I'm proud I joined the military. I'm the only female in my family who's done that. I'm also the only one that works on the railroad.

"Accomplishing anything and learning new things is always neat for me. My greatest accomplishment has been raising my kids so they're responsible adults.

"When the office jobs moved to Omaha, I had an option to go work on the Union Pacific side, but I decided to stay with UPFE. It's because I felt like I was leaving family. I'm a people person. I like working with the people I work with. I didn't want to start over someplace else. I work with a wonderful bunch of people.

"It has been an good experience for me, and I hope to continue doing it for as long as I can."

Transportation

Nancy Kohmetscher

"I hired out in 1990 and worked as a switchman (switchperson to be politically correct). I've been an engineer since 1995. Actually it was an accident that I began working for the railroad. I was working at a bank and wanted to do something different. I went down to the employment office and put my name in. Union Pacific interviews anyone with a 97 percentile average or above so they called me to come in for an interview. When they called, I didn't even know who the interview was for. After it was over, I kind of laughed thinking they'd never hire me. When they did, I thought I'd work until I got my college tuition but here I still am.

"I like the job. As far as the scheduling and things like that, it changes your life entirely. You're kind of once removed from the normal sector of society because of the hours—you know, the schedule that you keep. You're not able to make any plans or anything. That's rather difficult but the job itself is a good job.

"Sometimes as a woman you work twice as hard to be accepted as being able to do the work. Some of those social stigmas have gone away. There's still some there to a certain extent. We live in the midst of them. People don't accept women in professional jobs here as readily as they do in larger cities. It's gotten better but, yeah, it was difficult being someone who's totally not like everyone else—being out there and not being male and tall and strong physically. You look for your strengths. You acquire your knowledge. It doesn't come natural to you. But the railroad's changed a lot. They don't require a lot of that physical activity that they used to.

"It was pretty much on the job training. They put you out there. You had a trainer for a little while, then you went out there and did it. You learned from experience mostly. You learned from your mistakes.

"I really like the people I work with. People out there come from a lot of different walks of life. You might work with someone who is here from the East Coast. I've worked with a gentleman who was a world renowned photographer. He decided he was fed up with the rat race. He came back to the Midwest where he grew up and hired out switching. People like that have tremendous stories to tell. They're interesting to work with. I really enjoy that.

"My family does not like me working on the railroad. My family's old-fashioned. They don't think a woman should do man's work. They didn't like the idea at all.

"I plan to work for another ten years and then I hope to retire, get my senior discounts, and go to bingo."

Mary Gilmore

"I hired out on the railroad in June 1990 as a switchman/brakeman. At that time crews consisted of an engineer, conductor, and two brakemen. Everyone in my class went out on the road as brakemen. I chose to stay in the yard as a switchman as I had two children still at home. I was lucky to have that choice at the time.

"I was pretty intimidated at first, but most of the guys were pretty helpful and patient. I believe growing up with five brothers helped me in this male-dominated field.

"In 1993 I was able to go to engine service and became a qualified engineer in January 1994.

"I have enjoyed this job for the most part and am proud of my accomplishments. I had to quit recently due to health problems. I will miss the people and the freedom of being out on the road.

"I believe a woman hiring out on today's railroad will have a much easier time of it than when I hired out, as I'm sure my early days were easier for me than the women who hired out 10 to 15 years before me.

"Hats off to the first women of the railroad!"

Mary Gilmore, Engineer in Training 1993

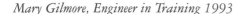

Frances Gledhill, Eva Melius, Donna Jones, Carol Wietzki, Carol Townsend, Mary Hanna (photo courtesy of Christy Callendar)

Mary Mooreland Hanna

"I started in April of '94 as a switchman/brakeman. I was Mary Mooreland then. At the time I started my daughter Jennifer went to the Navy and my son was almost out of high school, I needed a job with insurance. That's what I was after, insurance and retirement. A neighbor with two small children was working for the railroad. She said, 'I know you can do it, Mar.' That's what I did. I went out there and put in my application applying for transportation, fireman/oiler and apprentice electrician.

"Everybody starts on the third district going west up to South Morrill and going to Cheyenne when they can hold it. The only thing we haul up to South Morrill is coal. It's a real beautiful area up there. Sometimes when you're hauling coal, you go on the dark side to Egbert. The dark side is non-signaled territory. You have to get track warrants to go from milepost to milepost.

"I moved to the second district. The only thing I could hold over there was picker. That's the lowest paying job that's over there. When you're low on the stick that's where you get put.

"When it's a high-paying job, protected people take it. Protected persons get paid a high rate to get that train over the road quickly. They get paid a certain rate whether it takes them six hours or twelve hours. We got paid hourly but we got paid overtime. When it's a protected rate of pay they don't get overtime. Protected is anyone who was hired pre-'85. That's when they lost their brakemen and the caboose.

"When I was over on the second district, I married Richard Hanna. I had to stay over there if I was ever going to see him. We both worked as conductors on the Marysville run and then we went to school together. I've been an engineer since 1998. He came back as a conductor so we did get to work together.

"I enjoy working with people. The important thing is we need to work as a team. No matter if I'm wearing the hat of an engineer or a conductor, we need to work as a team. I enjoy working with all the new people and all the old heads because you can learn something every day. People don't think so, but you can. The new engineers that come out of school, they're learning all the new stuff that comes out. You can always learn stuff from the new kids coming in. You just got to be open-minded.

"Sometimes working all night gets a little rough. And the dirty bathrooms. I don't care for the dirty bathrooms. They come out of North Platte clean—reasonably clean—most of the time. But when you get them coming out of Marysville, they've already been clear back East somewhere. There are no firemen/oilers there to clean them. It's just a crew exchange. Crew gets off. Crew gets on. Whatever you've got, you've got. It's kind of like an outhouse. You just cover the pot and try to squat if possible.

"I used to work construction. I grew up on a farm. I'm used to hard work.

"I'm only had just a little derailment. Just a few wheels on the ground. Not a big derailment.

"I was on duty for 27 hours when we had that ice storm. We stopped and we slept for a while until a manager came and got us. By federal standards we can only work 12 hours but in an emergency status they can force us to work over 12 hours. We made it. There's nothing else you can do but try to do your best to get there safely.

"My daughter just started on the railroad. She also went into transportation. I wanted her to be a fireman/oiler but you know how children are.

"I'll probably stay on the Marysville run because it's a good run. It's beautiful once you turn south at Gibbon. There are lots and lots of trees and a lot of wildlife. You see mountain lions once in a while. Of course you see coyotes, foxes and a lot of deer. Bobcat too. Raccoons you see all the time and those nasty possums that are in the middle of the track eating. Sometimes those silly deer don't get out of the road very well. We do hit them and then they're lunch for whoever. The best thing is when it gets cold we see a lot of eagles. That's always a plus when it gets wintertime and early spring. They're beautiful.

"I appreciate my job and I don't take it for granted.

"I hope to stay healthy and take care of my grandchildren. I want to quilt at some point and to work in my yard and take care of my flowers—and go camping and fishing."

Carol Wietzki

"I've worked on ranches, been a weigh-master in a sale barn, a food waitress, owned my own beauty shop, cleaned houses, done day jobs driving cattle and moonlighted working calves at night. I've worked in a hayfield at harvest-time or plowed. I drove tractor hauling corn or beets. I've done lots of different jobs. I've never had a problem finding a job.

"One night my son Cole called and wouldn't back off until I promised to call a number.

"After I promised he said, 'It's a job on the railroad doing what I'm doing.'

"I said, 'I don't want to work on the railroad,' but he kind of backed me into a corner and here I am. I started working for Union Pacific in 1998.

"There are many things I like about being an engineer. My favorite part? I like to listen to the rhythm of a train. I really really enjoy that. I like to listen to the rhythm of the motor. Whether it's sitting there and I'm inside or outside, I pick up that rhythm. Or if we're lucky enough to get to run our speed. Right now I go east to Marysville. Coming home, as long as I can run my speed, I love it. And I like the people I work with.

"When you're as old as me working as a woman on the railroad, it's good. I don't mind it at all. I think the way a woman talks and the way that a woman acts is many times the way she's going to be treated. I've worked with some great people.

"In the wintertime in the cab it can get pretty cold. Things have changed but you can still freeze your tail off. We carry duct tape or white tape because a lot of the older units'll be airy around the doors or the back. In the summertime you've got air-conditioning unless you have an old, old unit. Or you're working picker or local—they might not have air-conditioning. If you're down on the ground that helps, but if you're the engineer you cook. It's hot. A picker is a train that stops and picks

Carol Wietzki

up cars and sets cars out—like at Gothenburg at Frito-Lay, they'll set out empties and pick up loads.

"When I was going through class they showed a video of all the things that can happen out there. Even though it was fake, that night I went to my motel room and I cried. A young guy in class who was my son's age tattled on me. He told the instructor and the instructor said, 'This is a dangerous job. You can kill somebody in a matter of seconds or you can be killed in a matter of seconds.' And he's right. That scared me.

"When I was in Cheyenne as a conductor we had to set out cars. It was wintertime. Middle of the night. Snow's blowing. I didn't know those yards very well because we rarely had to set cars out or pick them up there. My radio was working and not working—the battery was low. I walked ahead of the point of the shove looking for the switch. I saw it and said, 'Stop.' It was a switch with a foot pedal. There was snow but I knew where the switch was and I stepped on it. Normally I bent over and took the handle, but I stepped on that pedal. I felt it release. I didn't even have to touch it. There was so much pressure on the switch because we were so close. I felt the wind go by my face and that scared me. The switch handle would have hit me if I had leaned over. It would have killed me if it had hit me. Ninety-nine percent of the time I lean over and step, pull to the middle and step over and pull it over. Everybody out there has angels around them.

"I had a long fielder who worked down in one of the bowls tell me, 'If you're working out here at night and it's in the wintertime and you're walking between these rails, don't just look up high to see if there's a car coming. The ones that are going to kill you are shoulder-height.' The snow muffles all the sound and it will roll right over you. You'll never hear it coming. You have to be alert at all times. Between flesh and metal, metal's going to win.

"I hired on as switchman. After a three-week class, you're a conductor. Your job is to tie down cars (set the brakes), and to couple the cars if you're putting cars together. Anything on the ground that has to do with the cars is the conductor's job. If you derail or you go into emergency because you lose the air, the conductor gets out and walks the train and checks it. The engineer just runs it. The conductor does the ground work.

"I like riding the rail. I've gone in the yards two or three times but I'm not in there very long. I watch a train leave and emotionally I just leave with it. I like riding the train. I like the scenery going south to Marysville. Down along the river, it's winding. That's better than straight rail.

"Everybody's had some sort of close call or has hit somebody. Everybody's had the public play chicken with their train. The ones that do it know enough to pull off the rail when they hear you dump the air. That's when you'd like to get out and just beat the hell out of them because your heart's right up here. It's just up here.

"Or somebody goes through the gates. They have no idea how easily they can be killed.

"Or they've been flashed. Women flash you because they can't see inside the cab. It's happened to me twice. Once a couple on a motorcycle got really close and this girl just, you know. My conductor says, 'Did you see that?' If I'd only thought ahead, I'd have opened the window and waved.

"The first run is one you never forget. I wasn't nervous. I was fine. I was fine in the van. I was fine when I got my papers. I crawled on that train and we were in east departure one. I pulled down to the switches and stopped. We were waiting for the light to turn so we could start out on the main line. Everything goes through your mind even though you've been in there a hundred times. *What was the speed limit here? How fast can I go?* All of a sudden it just hits you—I'm running this. *Where's my counter? Where are my lights? Throttle. Independence. Air.* Everything's going through my mind all at once. *What if? What if? What was our speed? Are all of my switches lined correctly?* I was that way until we got out of town and all the lights were green. When I saw those green lights I was just good to go. The nervousness left like that. Before that it was almost like a brain freeze.

"Every trip is different because every train is different. I've worked around farm equipment. I've worked with horses and with horse hay equipment and trucks and pickups and trailers, but nothing in this world can prepare you for a 20,000 ton coal train. Nothing. And the weight you can feel pushing you is thrilling to me. There are spots where there can be derailment if you handle your train wrong. There are two or three spots that I may as well be alone in the cab—I like to focus that well to notch. I notch here. I notch out. I notch down. I do this. I do that. I'm eight thousand foot long or I'm twenty thousand three hundred and three tons heavy. It's almost like a game with myself to see if I can get through there and not feel run in, not feel run out. It's all that tonnage pushing you if you're going downhill. You can feel it and you can watch your accelerometer go.

"In a lot of ways it's an exciting job but there are days the boredom will drive you crazy when you're not moving. It's not just a physical fatigue because I could get out and walk. It's the emotional fatigue that drags you down. That's the hard part of the job. You might sit there for hours and not know why. Most of the dispatchers are pretty good, but some of the newer ones aren't very good at explaining why you're stopping.

"When we had the ice storm a couple of years ago all the signals went out. Some of the guys were out there 36 hours.

'I asked a young conductor one time, 'Did you not bring food?'

"'Yep,' he said, 'I have food. I was working out here with Brad Robbins when we had that ice storm. I didn't bring any food. Brad had an apple and a sandwich and he shared them with me. I was getting so hungry I started eating the hair off my arms.'

"That made me laugh all the way to Marysville.

"Going into Marysville...once for some reason I thought I should notch out. They say you feel your train by the seat of your pants, and I'm thinking, *My! I can feel it in my seat. It's almost like hydroplaning.* I looked down and my little yellow marble was buried. I thought, *My gosh, this could be serious.* I started notchin' back and notchin' back, and we get through Herkimer. There's a flashing yellow there. I had set I think ten pounds. I'm lookin' down. My little yellow marble, my accelerometer, is still way too fast. And you can feel it in the seat of your pants. It was the weirdest thing. We went flying by that flashing yellow at 52 miles an hour and it's downhill again. I set about twelve pounds the next time and it grabbed hold. It came right down. My conductor—he was a fairly quiet conductor—I thought either he's really quiet, or scared shitless. I should ask him some day if he had any idea.

It's things like that that make you remember. Every time I go down that hill I remember how easily that weight can push you and I stay on my toes, always alert to the PUSH of the train tonnage.

"This made me laugh so I saved it.
If your conductor wakes up, take initial.
If he stands up, go to full service.
If he jumps up, go to emergency!

"When I was working in the yards I redid the manuals. The old head yardmasters helped me with symbols. They had been copied so many times that they were a mess. We're always trying to improve the learning. When I started training as an engineer, I made a cheat sheet. I found out other guys had made themselves one. They shared their information. Ideas from everyone helps and protects others."

Stacey Tansey

Stacey has been with UPRR since 1998. She hired on a switchman in the transportation department. She has also worked as a peer trainer and as an RCL (Remote Control Locomotive) peer trainer. Stacey is currently a second district conductor.

Her advice to anyone considering working for the railroad, "It's a good career."

Stacey's mother Rose Roth works in the mechanical department. Stacey says, "Working for the same company helps us understand how each department affects the other."

Shawn Monk

"I was hired as a conductor in 2005. I previously worked electrical. I was at a point in my life where I needed benefits. Being on a single income for many years, I'd worked two or three jobs to survive, however working for the railroad has turned out to be probably more than two or three jobs. It's 24-hour a day, seven days a week regardless of weather conditions.

"I'm a single parent with a boy who was a junior in high school the year that I hired on. I was in the yard two years by choice. Money-wise it's not as good, but it's generally an eight-hour day so you're home with your family.

"On the train, the engineer is responsible for the power. The conductor is responsible for the cars. The conductor confirms that the train's ready to go, making sure for example, that there are no hazmat cars put on with a refrigerator-reefer car, which is a big no-no. Explosive cars have to be so many cars away from the power.

When you get on your train, you call the yardmaster on the radio to get permission to knock your brakes off and to leave the yard. You talk to the dispatcher that controls other parts of the yard you go through.

"When you get to the final destination, you get permission and yarding instructions from that yardmaster—things like which rail, if you tie it down, if you trade out with another crew, or if you have to get more power.

"Tying down a train means you tie the brakes so that when you leave the train, it doesn't go anywhere. You use a brake stick that looks kind of like a shepherd's crook. There's also a portable one that one of the conductors designed—it's about three foot long and you can make it another 18 inches longer. Sometimes the handbrakes are on the very tops of the cars—they're an older style brake. The brakes on most of the cars look like the steering wheel of a car.

"In Bailey Yard you tie a minimum of five brakes. Up at Morrill it's three, but they have a concave rail that's higher on the ends and sinks down in the middle so the train can't roll out either end. On a loaded train you still tie at least five brakes up there. After you tie them, the engineer does a release to see if you have enough brakes to hold. If it's a real heavy train you have to tie more—you tie as many as it takes. The Gerald Gentlemen station in Sutherland is kind of an uphill climb. I tied 18 brakes there one day.

"You walk a train when you have a problem. It's a lot more comforting if it's daylight or you have a big ol' moon. The lantern doesn't shed much light when it's pitch black. There are a lot of animals out there—a lot of coyotes, and mountain lions have walked right up to the train. Badgers seem to like to live under the tracks—soft digging for them I guess. The biggest train I've ever had was around 149 cars which is roughly a mile and a half.

"When you're walking the train you're looking for the reason it's come apart or gone into emergency. It's usually because you lost your air. Or it could be a knuckle. Knuckles kind of lock like two c's that collapse together. There are pin lifters that lift those knuckles. Sometimes if you hit a rough crossing it may come apart. It might not be broken. I've only had a broken knuckle once in five years. If it's knuckles that came apart, you get the engineer to back the train back together.

"Sometimes you walk the train because you get a defect. They have detectors roughly every 20 miles along the track that'll tell you exactly which car it is, the axle number and which side of the car that it's on. We haven't been trained to work on cars. All we can do is go and see if we know what the problem is. An old head trainman told me to take zip ties. If the hose was dragging too low and got pulled apart, you take a couple of zip ties and bring it up.

"I've seen several hoboes. One day a guy jumped out of an empty coal car. He took off running like he was scared to death—like someone was chasing him. Nobody was.

"The other instance it was raining and the wind was blowing so hard it had to be horrible to be out in it. I came across Birdwood Crossing and saw something black and billowy up in the road ahead of me. Between the hard rain and the dark I couldn't tell what it was until I got almost on top of it. It was a nun. It looked like a male version of a nun with the full headpiece. The long skirt was billowing all over. He jumped out right in front of me. He or she. A very manly looking woman if it was one. There was another person dressed as a priest—hiding down in the ditch peeking up at me to see if I was going to stop. I didn't because I didn't want soaking wet strangers covered with coal dust in my car. Normally I'm a good samaritan but that day I just wasn't. But I'm positive it was two men. I'm sure that they'd gotten off the train.

"Right now the only route I can hold is Morrill, the lowest in the seniority run. It's a preferred run for a lot of the old conductors because the coal cars are newer and don't give you as many problems.

"It's a very pretty route. You don't know what pretty is until you see the sun come up and the moon go down.

You wouldn't believe the amount of wildlife that there is in Nebraska. One night there were probably 1200 deer. Turkeys come right up when the trains are stopped. They don't fly up. They walk up. And be right on top of the power. The noise doesn't discourage them at all.

"Even after working on a Navy base and working construction and other jobs around a lot of men, I would say it's a little bit of a chauvinistic environment. I think men are a little, maybe intimidated, that women can do the job that the men do. Maybe a little old-fashioned. A lot of them are older men and maybe think women belong at home.

"The toughest part to me is keeping up with all the rules. Another issue is the weight that goes with it. The grip is so heavy and not only do you have to lift it, you have to lift it over your head to the top step of the power before you climb up.

"I've got a backpack that's got very little in it that's not railroad related; a calculator, the emergency stuff that I have if I have to walk a train; a bag with the axle counter; a wax stick to stick up to the wheel if it feels hot to your hand. The wax stick is like a big Sharpie pen with wax in it. If it melts, you definitely have to set the car out. You mark which axle it is. You initial it and date it. Of course it's got the zip ties, bad order tags and magic markers and all my paper work. I go different directions sometimes so I might carry both Cheyenne and Morrill paperwork. We have what they call general orders for each territory. Those are mandatory to carry with you. You have a hazmat book and a safety book you have to have with you at all times. You have your g-cor (General Code of Rules) binder that must weigh five pounds. Some people have those on their phones or their pda's but now that we can't have electronic devices, we'd have to stop your train in order to be able to use them.

"When I hired on there were roughly 12 in my hire class—only two females. It's certainly not that they're not looking for women to work in the craft. It's more that to qualify, you have to be strong enough to do the work. As far as the test, I think it was tough for everybody, male or female.

"I've a got a bachelor's. Someday I might try for a management position but right now I'm ok with working on the train. The hours could be better; it could be a cleaner job; if it was daylight or a full moon when I had to walk the train that would be good. I don't think anybody likes walking the train at night, male or female.

"I like my job. I was never scared of the work because I was a farm girl and around equipment all my life. We crossed the tracks going into town and it never ever occurred to me that women worked for the railroad."

Frances Gledhill

"I was hired in the 2006 hiring fair. My kids kept saying, 'Mom, just go and try.'

I thought I was too old to think about changing careers, but I said, 'Ok. I'll do it. We'll see if they can hire an old lady.'

"I passed all the tests and was hired on the spot. I passed my physical and they put me through a lot of classes. I learned to operate remotes—the box you carry on your vest. Remotes operate locomotives that don't have that conductor or an engineer in there.

Frances Gledhill (photo courtesy of Christy Callender)

"It's a great job. I used to count train cars when I was a little kid. I never dreamed I would be up inside one of those locomotives as a conductor. My goal is to continue until I'm at least sixty-five or I have to have a cane to get up on the locomotive.

"When I'm not working as a conductor, or laid off as I am currently, I'm on the AWR, a reserve board. It keeps you employed with benefits, but you only work two days a week.

"It is a man's world, but there are a lot of women now.

"My family lives here so I stay here. I do borrow out, which is a great opportunity that they give you. I just got back from Laredo, Texas. I worked in the yard there. It's still Union Pacific, but you learn different ways that people do stuff.

"My first borrow out was to Saint Louis. That was awesome. I saw other parts of the country and met other engineers and conductors.

"I went to Rawlins, Wyoming. It's a place I wouldn't want to go back to but we help them when they're in short demand of employees.

"You have to have your mind set on work when you go to work. If you take it off just for that one second and forget to look both ways, then it's devastation. You can't hear cars rolling in the bowl. People kept telling me that. I thought, *Well that's a lot of tonnage. You're going to hear something.* But, no. In the wintertime you just don't hear the cars coming at you.

"They take extra safety precautions. They block off a rail if you're working in a rail. You have to wear jeans. I keep my hair tucked back out of my way. If you wear a coat you have it tight under your chin so it's not blocking your vision. No one wants to have an accident out there.

"I don't like is pulling pins. That's up on what we call the hump. It's doing the same thing over and over. You have a train coming up the hill. You pull a pin as it crests. It rolls down the hill. Once you release it, it goes to a certain track where they build a train. It's a simple job if you know what you're doing and keep your mind focused.

"The car does not stop while you're pulling that pin. You walk beside it. It's going about four miles per hour. You just grab hold of the pin. You can let go of it, but if the pin falls back down then you have to stop the cars. I've had to stop the cars many times—either I miss a pin or I miss the point at where I can pull the pin. You don't come out with a pin in your hand. I call it a pin but it's a big bar. It's kind of heavy. You pull on it and it lifts up the knuckle. It releases the knuckle where it opens up.

"I am sore sometimes when I do it because we do at least two trains a shift and some of the trains have a hundred and twenty cars. My last time up on the hill it was minus forty degrees. I thought my fingers were going to fall off every time I pulled the pin. You keep going. They have a quota to meet. They can't shut down.

"I think a lot of men have gained a lot of respect for the women out there now. They've accepted us more. I know a lot of them get tired of having to train because it seems like they have somebody with them all the time. Some of them think it's babysitting, but they know we're not there to take their job, but just to have a job like them and support our families.

"I don't like working in the yard. I love the people, but I'm ready to get back on a train and be a conductor again. That's my passion, being on the train.

"In my class we started out with five women. We have three left. A hiring session is considered a class. You train with your class. We're basically all done at the same time, and let loose at the same time, and put on the board at the same time. It's about three months before you're actually out on your own.

"They have peer trainers you can call to come and help you. Because the yard is so big, I had to call and find out how to get to my first job. All the jobs are spread out. I thought I'd never learn the yard. Now it's like a piece of cake getting around. Once you know where you're going and what you're doing, it's easy, but when you're

out there looking at it the first time, you're in awe.

"It's hard to get used to being on call twenty-four hours a day, seven days a week. You just get to sleep and the phone's ringing. I don't have to worry about my family. My kids are full-grown.

"My granddaughter thinks it's awesome that I'm out riding the train. I'll be fifty-five this year and I'm still climbing up on locomotives. I think that's pretty good.

"It's an awesome job. Every day I walk out there think, 'Wow, what a job! I get to play with trains all day.'

"There's an alerter button in the cab engine. It comes on to make sure there's somebody manning the train. If there's no response, the train goes into emergency. It doesn't jar the train. It gradually cuts the brakes and you stop. You have to let your air come back before you can go again. It seems like it takes forever but it only takes maybe ten minutes.

"My job as a conductor is to watch the lights. I have to call out, 'Ok, you've got a clear.' Or a flashing yellow. Flashing yellow means the next is going to be a solid yellow. You'll be stopping at the one after that.

"If the train breaks apart, it's my job to walk the train and find out why it came apart and put it back together. Usually it's an air hose that's either come loose or broken, or a jolt broke the knuckle. We have two knuckles that are on the locomotives, but to carry them back... you hope and pray another train comes by and they'll

Frances Gledhill (photo courtesy of Christy Callender)

stop. I haven't heard of anybody carrying a knuckle very far yet. It'll be challenging if I'm on a train that breaks apart and I have to replace the knuckle by myself. You have to be able to lift eighty-five pounds in order to be hired because knuckles weigh up to eighty-five pounds. For a female I think that's challenging. There are people that will help you. I've been lucky in the yard. There's always been a male to help put it on.

"I have a conductor's log book. I write down every light we go through. That way they know you were awake.

"A lot of people have been issued brake sticks. With a brake stick you can tie your hand brakes from the ground and you don't have to climb up each car. If you get ice that's thick because it's melted and frozen or you get icicles on the grip bars, it can get kind of scary.

"You have to have a lantern to give signals in the yard at night. Union Pacific furnishes your lanterns—and your gloves. We go through gloves every two months or so because they get so black and dirty from the locomotives. Before you catch yourself, you wipe your face and get black all over it. Or you get hot and start brushing your forehead and get black all over your forehead.

"I really enjoy working there and I enjoy borrowing out."

Christy White Miller

"My seniority date is June 20, 2006. I'm a certified conductor, switchman and engineer. Right now I'm holding a switchman job because I like to stay in the yard. What got me out to the railroad was the health insurance and the pay. They pay their women the same as they do their men. You don't get that everywhere and nowhere else in North Platte as a woman, unless you have like a doctor's degree, are you going to get a job that pays that well.

"I went to Salt Lake to class. There were six of us, the most women they've ever had in a class. When we're off we're still trained at tech school at Mid-Plains so we're kept up to date and can just go back to work.

"Right now there are maybe 50 women in transportation. We kind of stick together like a pack which is great. You get help with little things like where's a clean bathroom.

"You do feel like it's a man's world. You line switches. You're outside in freezing weather at midnight when it's 20 below. You're like, *I should be at home baking cookies and getting kids ready for school* but you're out there working with the men. I'm proud of myself for being

able to go out there and bear the cold. That's a sense of accomplishment for me. Sometimes the colder it is and the rainier it is and the stormier it is, the faster your work goes and the more exciting it is.

"It's a man's world because you don't see a lot of prissy things. You don't get to sit in an office. You're out there working and moving power and building trains—building America, as they say.

"When you go to work you have to wear steel-toed workboots and jeans and you can't wear v-necked shirts for safety reasons. You have to have earplugs and you have to wear safety glasses so when you're a girl and you go to work out there you just want to bring a little bit of your girl with you. I always wear barrettes—a red one...a pink one...it might be big... it might be little. Or a hat. My winter hats are always a big deal for me. My husband always makes fun of me, 'Well, it's just to keep you warm,' he says, but I have to look good too because there's nothing else that looks good that I wear to work.

"Sometimes as a girl you feel like you have to prove to the guys that you can do it. They don't make you feel this way but you do feel this way because you're so outnumbered by men. You try ten times harder. You're doing everything you possibly can. You know in your own mind that you can do it and you don't want to ask anybody for help because it might show just a little bit of weakness. Never have I ever had that feeling that I didn't belong there. Everybody treats you equally and believes in you, and believes that you can do the job just as well as they do. You just got to prove it to yourself.

"My Grandpa Hunt worked in the shop when they used to have family days out at the railroad. They let us crawl on the locomotive and I remember thinking, *This is the coolest thing ever!* As a child I thought I'd like to ride on a locomotive and now I'm doing it.

"My favorite job is to work power to the yard. That means I take the power (that's slang for locomotive) and line the switches to build a train. There are 64 bull rails. They're lined with cars that have been humped. I have a list of car numbers and I go in and out of the rails to build my train. I switch over different cars to different rails and pull them down to the departure gate. I ride the point sometimes. That means I ride on the front end of the locomotive or the trailing end, depending on which way the locomotive's facing, east or west, and whether it's going to east departures or west. I call and get permission to get onto certain tracks. The hostler runs the power and I line the switches all the way down to the departure tracks. Riding the point on a summer night when it's 70 degrees outside and the stars are out is a thrill. Then I look back and I see the whole train that I helped build. That's a pretty cool accomplishment. I like being able to tell my kids, 'Your mom builds trains.'

"I've been an engineer and that's quite the experience to run a whole train. When you get your work orders to run a train to Cheyenne or South Morrill, your name is on that paperwork. It will say Owner of Train. That is your train. If anything happens, that's your train you just broke. When you look in your side mirror and you can see a two-mile long train, you're thinking, *I've got a lot of responsibility on my hands.* And reading all the lights? It's pretty exciting to know that I can do that. You have to go through a lot of training. You got to know your rules. I carry a backpack every day and it's got my rule book, my timetables, and my PPE—that's personal protective equipment—safety glasses, earplugs, safety vest, gloves, lantern. I love my lantern. That lantern is a critical part of your job. You lose your lantern and you're frantic. You always remember the first lantern you ever got. I carved Princess into mine so none of the guys would steal it. And your pens are important because you write orders with them. I always take pink pens because I know they're not going to get stolen.

"For a long time my kids didn't even know I had a job. I worked midnights so I'd put them to bed and go to work and by the time I got home it was time to get them up and get them ready for school. I got them out the door and went to sleep. When I woke up it was time to pick them up from school. My son said to me one day, 'Aren't you ever going to get a job?'"

"In order to be a hostler in North Platte you have to be a certified engineer. My seniority would qualify me to be a conductor. It's a way easier job, but you're out of town all the time. I'm about four or five people away from being a hostler so when they add out to the road, I'm going to be hostling.

"When you get bumped you have 48 hours to mark up on a different job. That's kind of nice since you get some time off without having to lay off. There are so many different jobs out there and there are many that I'm qualified to do.

"I love my job. When I was first hired it seemed overwhelming and I was nervous but I learned I can do it."

Remote Control Locomotives (RCLs)

A remote control locomotive (RCL) is one that can be operated by a person using a radio transmitter and receiver system. The operator need not be in the cab of the locomotive. Safety designs automatically stop the locomotive if communication with the controller is lost.

In the United States, this technology is mostly confined to yard operations, but it has been implemented on a wider scale in Canada. In the United States the Federal Railroad Administration (FRA) is assessing data of all operations to ensure that RCLs pose no threat to railroad workers or to the public.

In 2001 FRA issued a Notice of Safety Advisory which was published in the Federal Register. The advisory is a nonregulatory approach in delivering guidance to the rail industry on how, in FRA's view, these operations should be conducted.

Concerns centered around:

- operations in bad weather
- ergonomic issues in the design of the remote control transmitter (RCT)
- electromagnetic field (EMF) emissions from RCTs
- insufficient clearance when wearing the RCTs in tight spaces
- roadway worker protection issues
- mental and physical stress associated with RCL operation
- lack of accurate exposure metrics for calculating accident rates

Advantages included:

- better visual contact with the leading end of rail movements,
- the elimination of communication error between the locomotive engineer and ground crew
- the reduction of yard accidents and injuries

FRA noted that data comparing the safety of remote control and manual operations has been difficult to obtain and that more data is needed.

"As this new technology expands, the continued input of the men and women who operate RCLs will be necessary to ensure that ergonomic issues and operating concerns are properly identified and fully addressed, consistent with the needs of both RCOs and the rail industry.

"Furthermore, we must be cognizant that gender specific issues may arise with respect to ergonomic challenges and solutions. FRA will, therefore, recommend that railroads give special consideration to the unique human/machine interface problems that may arise during the proliferation of this technology particularly regarding female operators."

The last sentence is a most telling indication of how far women have come in the rail industry.

Management

Jennifer Fuller

"I started working for Union Pacific January 5, 2005. I started out as clerk. That's an agreement job. I became a dispatcher, which is non-agreement, one year after that. I moved to corridor manager one year ago. I love my job. It's different every day.

"I come from a railroad family. I have six uncles and they all work for the railroad as well as my dad. They're all very proud of me.

Jennifer Fuller (photo courtesy of Morgan Greenwood)

"I plan to continue working for the railroad. I plan to continue moving up and enjoying my job.

"Being a corridor manager consists of lots of things. I watch trains coming in and out of the yard. I watch trains being built to be sure they're built correctly. I make sure trains have power and that the crews have enough time to get into the yard and do their work. I test dispatchers to make sure they're doing their jobs correctly. I work with yardmasters, directors, and superintendents to make sure everything is running smoothly in Bailey Yards.

"We use computer-aided dispatching, the cad system. We have multiple screens to watch the trains go across our territory. Cameras are placed out in the yard so we can see what's going over the humps and the trim. We make sure everything is safe. We use a lot of computers to do our job.

"I think it's important to enjoy your job. You should always keep your family first, but enjoy your job and give it all you have because it's worth it. It's very rewarding.

"I moved back to North Platte from Omaha after college. One of my uncles who's a retired manager said, 'They're hiring clerks.'

"I said, 'I will never live in North Platte and I will never work for the railroad.'

"Then I said, 'Ok, I guess I'll apply.'

"I got hired.

"I moved really fast. I was janitor for this building, emptying the trash, supplying water for the crews, emptying the recycle bags and cleaning the restrooms. That's what I did when I first got hired. I went from being a janitor to a timekeeper to a yard office supervisor within six months. My sixth month I became the clerk for this office. Six months later I became a dispatcher. A year later I became corridor manager. You know it just changed so fast. I went from being a janitor to running the trains.

"It's an amazing feeling to run the whole yard. I give all the signals. I give all the switches. It's empowering to know that I'm doing all that. My uncle told me to apply and I did.

"I've had awesome, awesome opportunities. I've always give 100%. I think when you give 100%, people see that. Every time there's been an opportunity, I've been given that opportunity. I'm very blessed. I love my job. I don't take it for granted a single day. I work for good people. I have a great boss. It's just good."

Mary Manero

Mary Manero is Manager of Terminal Operations. She started with Union Pacific in 2004 as a billing specialist for Transcentric then went into the manager training program. She was manager of yard operations in Fremont before coming to North Platte.

"The management program includes rules training and some training on the ground doing exactly what conductors and engineers do. It has a lot as far as the communication piece. It's an accelerated management course. We teach you what you need to know to start running the yard. The standard management program is a year long, but people can be promoted anywhere from six months to a year.

"I never had a fascination with trains until I got here. I spent time in the military and in accounting type positions after the military. I knew that I was bored. I didn't like the office jobs, the four walls or a cubicle. I saw an ad in Kansas City. It just clicked completely that that was what I wanted. Since I've joined UP I've never looked back. I can't imagine going anywhere else.

"The biggest part of my day is communication. I supervise yardmasters and locomotive supervisors who in turn supervise our transportation and yard crews. They supervise the diesel mechanics, machinists, and electricians that service the locomotives. I basically supervise the supervisors. Probably the best part of the job is that I get out and talk to people. I get to know them. I talk to them about working safely. I talk to them about how they're doing their job and ask them how I can help make their job better.

"Coming to a new place, it doesn't take long for people to figure out who you are. If you know what you're doing and you treat people fairly, then you're just one of the managers and it doesn't matter that you're female or not. You're just one of them. That's not such a barrier any more.

"I try to do some mentoring with the new women coming up through the ranks. One of the things that I tell them is, 'The only thing that limits you is yourself and your own dreams. Wherever you want to go with this company, you can do it. It make take a little work, a little effort, a little bit of time, but anything is possible if you're only limited by what you want to do yourself.'

"I have learned that I really do like mentoring. I like to be in a role where I'm very involved in the training of the new managers because I think that has a major effect in how we're going to change the culture of the company. I've already seen changes here in North Platte. We've gotten away from the 'do this because I told you to.' We communicate well with our crews.

"We work on building relationships. I can go out and talk to the people who work with me or for me and get to know them. I get to know something of their fam-

Mary Manero's boots (photo courtesy of Morgan Greenwood)

ily—what's going on in their lives that may affect how they work here. When you get to know the people, you do much better relationships. Your work force is happier and you get a lot more done—and you get it done safely. North Platte is doing a great job with that.

"There are lots of opportunities for training and classes. We require forty hours of training every year in leadership, rules and skills, and communication skills. I take as much as they'll let me have each year because I know that there's always something to benefit from a class.

"My hours are fairly predictable. I've had jobs with UP in the past where they were not. Here I work a twelve-hour day. If I'm on day shifts, it starts at 5:45 A.M. and I finish about 6:15 P.M. When I work night shifts it's just the opposite. I work five days a week with two off. I don't have to work around family schedules so much anymore. My husband is retired. Both of my children are in Omaha. When I started they were old enough to care for themselves, however I don't think I could have done it without the support I had at home. My husband was a stay-at-home dad. With all the night shifts and time and the phones ringing all hours, it really, really helped to have him there. He supported what I did because he knew how much I loved it. It helped to have him there because even if you have really good teenagers, you still need somebody there with a thumb on them. With any age kids, you need some kind of support like that.

"I would give women the same advice I give my children. 'Figure out what you're passionate about, what you love to do, and then figure out how to make it work. Once you figure that out, the sky's the limit.' That's the way I feel here at Union Pacific. I'm so happy with what I do. I have opportunities every single day to learn something new and to be challenged by something. For me, it's an awesome career. I couldn't imagine being anywhere else or working for another company.

"There are two of us women who work out in the yard with the crews as managers. On the North Platte Service Unit we have in the range of 100 women, give or take 20 each way, in all departments. That includes those who are in the North Platte Service Unit but not here, but in say Marysville, or South Morrill.

"Union Pacific has an organization for women called LEAD (Lead, Educate, Achieve, and Develop). When I came a year ago, we didn't have a chapter so I started that. We're still a pretty young group. We have 24 members. LEAD helps women achieve whatever they want. If they want specific training, we try and do it for them. It's also a group that does charitable events for the community. It's a nice support system.

"LEAD is a great organization. The conferences are wonderful. Our superintendent here gives us one hundred percent support. When I told him I wanted to start a LEAD chapter, he was like, 'Absolutely!' He was one of the very first who signed up because it's not exclusive to women memberships.

"I never realized how much I love trains. I got involved in Operation Lifesaver because as a manager I see the emotional toll it takes on our guys when we have a crossing accident and we hit somebody. You know, they made a decision when they were on our tracks. Our guys can't avoid that. They can't swerve. I wanted to get involved in Operation Lifesaver so that I could at least educate the public about how dangerous crossings can be; how fast trains can move; how hard it is for us to stop for them. Maybe we can reduce the emotional toll on our guys.

"For women there still is that initial thing... that you have to prove that you can do it. But it doesn't take long. Once you do that, the guys out here are great. They have great respect for the women out here who work alongside of them. I don't see a huge issue with that.

"I don't get any grief. My co-managers treat me just like they do everyone else. I've been challenged as far as being a new manager, as far as knowledge and skills, but I don't think it's because I'm a woman. I think it's because I'm a new manager. I see it happen with the new young male managers also. They get that same kind of challenge. The crews out here want to know that we know what we're doing and what we're talking about. I'm not singled out. I'm part of the team. I like that.

"I've had people say, 'Are you really for real?' because I do have passion. But then you have to learn to balance it too. When I first started I didn't have a whole lot of balance. Everything was work. Sixteen, eighteen hour days, I'd go home and worry about it, sleep, and wake up thinking about it. Now it's better. I have a little more flexibility in my actual day. I'm here for twelve and gone.

"I get asked, 'You left headquarters Monday through Friday, eight-to-five, to come out to this?' Absolutely. And I never looked back. I think I might be back there one day because I want to do that mentoring and training and coaching piece that I feel so strongly about. That's the place to do it. But until then, I'm having way too much fun out here."

Top Row, left to right: *Maegan Petersen, Frances Gledhill, Waneita Schomer, Twila Bryoff, Donna Fair, Deb Tanner, Rita Dobbins, Mary Hanna, Rhonda Quaney*

Middle Row, left to right: *Pam Talmage, Eva Melius, Misti Brown, Donna Jones, Dorothy Savory, Carol Townsend, Carol Wietzki, Kristy Lage*

Bottom Row, left to right: *Marjorie Taylor, Thelma Wilson, Dorothy Davis, Marilyn Maseberg, Darlene Siegmann, Mary Gilmore, Tena Craghead, Pauline Maxwell*

Photo courtesy of Christy Callendar 2011

Six Generations of Railroaders

The women included in this book span the years from 1907 to 2011. Genevieve Jeffers opens the era of employment of women and her great-great-granddaughter Christy Miller brings it to the present day, but Christy's railroading family goes back even further—she comes from a six-generation-long line of railroaders.

Christy's great-great-great grandfather was Anthony Jeffers. Born in 1840 in Swinford Ireland County Mayo, Anthony was the youngest of the Jeffers family in Ireland. The British took over their land when he was eight and the family was forced to leave their potato farm. Anthony was taken to another farm and hidden in a barn since he was too young to work. The barn caught fire and he was burned. He was moved to another farm where he was healed and put to work. The landlord there had a daughter Susan who took lunch to the workers. Though warned to stay away from Anthony, she fell in love and the two of them were married and crossed the ocean to the United States. Anthony found work in a bar in Kansas.

Unknown to Anthony, his brother William had also come from Ireland and was working for the Union Pacific in North Platte. (William was the father of Bill Jeffers who became president of the Union Pacific.) When a man in North Platte told William he'd met a barman named Anthony Jeffers, William told him to tell the barman if he had a brother William he should come to North Platte and work on the railroad. In 1865 Anthony and Susan came to North Platte and Anthony hired on with Union Pacific.

Anthony's son Thomas Edward Jeffers was Christy's great-great-grandfather. He was superintendent of Union Pacific's store department. He retired in 1943 after 47 years of service.

The oldest of Thomas's twelve children, Genevieve, was Christy's great-grandmother. She was one of the first women to work for Union Pacific in North Platte, hiring on as assistant store helper when she was 16. While working for Union Pacific, Genevieve met William "Ike" Easton, a switchman, and fell in love. She and Ike were married in 1920 and Genevieve quit work to raise a family. Ike retired as an engineer after 40 years with Union Pacific. Together they raised eight children: Geraldine, William, Robert, Florence, Bonnie, Richard, Mary, and David.

Besides Christy's great-grandparents Genevieve and Ike, Christy's grandfather James Hunt worked at Union Pacific. James was the husband of Genevieve's youngest daughter Mary. He worked as an electrical foreman for 32 years, retiring in 1986.

Christy's father Joe White worked in the diesel shop from 1975 to 1979.

Christy is employed as a switchman and is a certified engineer, conductor and hostler,

Sharing the family tree with Genevieve's great-granddaughter Christy are two granddaughters: Patty Morris Smith who was employed as carmen foreman and Kim Easton Oltman who was a yardmaster, plus many, many male railroaders. Though a number of families have a railroading heritage, few can claim six generations with four women in the lineage.

Anthony Jeffers

Thomas Jeffers

Genevieve Jeffers

Thomas Jeffers and his family
Genevieve in back row 3rd from left

Young Genevieve and Ike

Older Genevieve and Ike

James Hunt

Joe White

Christy Miller

More Photos from the 1940s

Katie Tatom Deidel Paul and Helen Tatom Beisner

Pauline Jones, Goldie and Martha Johansen, & unknown

Red B., Red Campbell, Johnson, unknown,Gary Stinnette, Grace Smith and Marjorie Taylor

Mark Fletcher, Bob Stearns, Helen Beisner, James Adams

Union Pacific's Equal Employment Opportunity Policy

Union Pacific provides equal opportunity to all employees and applicants, without regard to race, color, gender, national origin, age, religion, sexual orientation, veteran status or disability.

Our policy exceeds federal and state Equal Employment Opportunity laws and applies to all terms and conditions of employment – including, but not limited to, hiring placement, promotion, demotion, termination, transfer, leaves of absence, compensation and training.

We are committed to affirmative action (PDF File) for women, minorities, individuals with disabilities and veterans at all levels and in every segment of our workforce.

Although this policy provides a good foundation for equal opportunity, Union Pacific believes that defining diversity goes beyond the current legal definitions of protected classes. In addition to differences of race, color, gender, national origin, age, religion, veteran status and disability status, diversity encompasses marital status, family status, political affiliations, educational background, socioeconomic status, lifestyle, sexual orientation, disabilities and other non-job-related factors.

A discrimination-free workplace and fair treatment are fundamental rights of all Union Pacific employees. Our work environment must always be one that respects and values differences – so that we may all contribute to our fullest potential.

Union Pacific's Harassment Policy

We are committed to providing a work environment free from offensive behavior directed at a person's race, color, national origin, religion, gender, sexual orientation, age, veteran status or disability. That includes behavior toward other employees, customers, visitors to company facilities, and anyone employees come in contact with during the normal course of work or while representing the company.

http://www.unionpacific.jobs/careers/working/culture/eeo.shtml

Johanna Johnson, Marie Brown, Katie Deidel, Pauline Jones, Florence Williams, Gladys Kariger
(1940s photo courtesy of Marjorie Taylor)

Railroad Terminology

Big hole the train - throw the emergency brakes on the train

Blocking a train - putting cars of the same destination together to make a new train

Buckle - hook the air hoses between cars together

Bulletin a job - put a job out for solicitation for bids

Bumped - someone with more seniority bid your job and got it

Bumped in - took a job by replacing someone with less seniority

Cab alley - area where the cabooses used as temporary housing sat

Car toad - carman

Distributive power - a locomotive or group of locomotives entrained or at the rear of a train and remotely controlled from the lead locomotive of a train. Not the same as Remote Control Locomotives

Do a roll-by - inspect a passing train when your train is stopped for a light or a signal. Includes listening for a klunk, klunk, klunk (bad wheel) and watching for sparks (hand brake on a car on)

Dynamite the train - throw the emergency brakes on the train

Dump the train - lock the brakes

Foamers - rabid railroad fans

FRA - Federal Regulatory Agency

FRED - blinking box attached to the back of a train when there's no unit back there

Go on the dark side - travel where warrants are needed to advance from milepost to milepost

Grip - luggage bag

High-spotting - creeping up in speed, like going 65 or 70 when the clearance is 60 mph

Hoghead - engineer

Humpers - hoboes

Humping trains - sending cars to different locations

LEAD (Lead, Educate, Achieve, and Develop) - Union Pacific's women's organization

Lid - inexperienced telegraph operator

Lightning slingers - telegraph operators

Notch up or down - Shift

Old Head - person with a lot of seniority

On the extra board - no regular assignment but available to be called

RCL - Remote Control Locomotive

The most whiskers - the most seniority

The power - the locomotive

Tricks -

    First trick - daytime shift

    Second trick - afternoon shift

    Third trick - night shift

TTD - Terminal Train Dispatcher

Wahoo in the train - freight car headed for the wrong destination on the wrong train

Wheeler - list of cars on a train

List of Women Featured in *Powering UP*

The Women of *Powering UP* in the order that they appear in the book:

SECTION I — The Women of World War I
to 1941

McCoy, Minnie
Lowe, Lena Wangen
Stamp, Florence
Brodbeck, Alma
Paul, Catherine Tatom Beloit Deidel
Shaw, Maude Miller Campbell Hall
Easton, Genevieve Jeffers
Gleeson, Margaret
Frye, Ethel A.
Kiehm, Beulah McGraw
Davis, Pansy L.
Babbit, Jessie
Hinman, Dorothy C.
McWilliams, Minerva
Merrill, Peryle Hunter
Brodbeck, Elmyra W.
Hayes, Vanita M.
Estermann, Jessie Joy Baker Hughes
Birk, Marion Faulkner
George, Mary Elias
Fonda, Blanch M.
Halligan, Louise Ottenstein
Schlientz, Mary L.
Schwaiger, Esther

SECTION II — The Women of World War II
to 1960

Taylor, Marjorie Hartford Halverson
Essley, Grace Smith
Davis, Dorothy Campbell
Stearns, Helen Engleman
Kariger, Gladys
Smith, Kathryn Kariger
Daharsh, Bertha Kariger
McEntire, Dollie
Faught, Loretta Schnitker Baker
Shinley, Leila Surber
Slattery, Margaret Hassenstab
Snyder, Mary Flynn
Beisner, Helen Tatom
Lum, Goldie Johansen
Merrell, Martha Johansen
Johanson, Dorothy
Johnson, Johanna C.
Jones, Pauline
Kirts, Zelma

Frake, Matilda (Tillie) Sands
McCulla, Alma
Stephens, Jessie
Hensley, Ilene
Naude, Bess
Cline, Elsie
Hultquist, Hazel
Baker, Ruth Ogborn Larson
Smith, Lola
Williams, Florence
Dedmore, Hattie Gardner
Brown, Marie Traudt Stone Kohl
White, Katherine Hartford Slattery
Beardsley, Evelyn
Motsinger, Ruth
Thompson, Martha
Kunc, Josephine Kovanda
Halsey, Viola Atteberry
White, Viola
McGovern, Bonnie Pendergast
Schaeffer, Mary Hunter
Ickes, Mildred Majer Stacy
Guilliame, Lillian (Billie) Powell
Gruball, Evelyn Powell
Jergensen, Mildred Swift
Brown, Edna Gifford Moser
Kosbau, Maxine Estes
Stack, Wilma
Griffith, Margaret Carothers
McPeak, Billie J
Thomsen, Viola Schmidt Cool
Maseberg, Marilyn
Dunn, Marianne Dolan Wallace
Ricketts, Arlene Boggs
Wilson, Thelma Hill
Miller, Frances Kemper
Edwards, Lena Flock
Walter, Frances Bradley
Schomer, Waneita
Maxwell, Pauline Hora
Gale, LeNore Fletcher Weekly
Durham, Margaret
Thalken, Alice Fitzpatrick Blalock
Rutt, Helene Rehn
Mattke, Pennie
Drummy, Jane L.
Gorman, Irene Cummings

SECTION III — The Women of Affirmative
Action to 1990

Branting, Bonny Mitchell
Siegmann, Darlene Clemens
Johansen, Joan
North, Bonnie
Noonan, Judy
Strawn, Betty Anne Parr
Martin, Janice
Brynoff, Twila
Jones, Donna
Pierson, Gwen Foust
Miller, Anne
Lage, Kristy Baade
Townsend, Carol
Justus, Edwina (Curly)
Pfortmiller, Diane
Tanner, Deborah Dancer
Quaney Rhonda Putnam Steffes
Dobbins, Rita Aylward
Tuenge, Shirley Mitchell
Best, Jody
Fair, Donna

SECTION IV — The Women of Today

Hansen, Brenda
Foster, Mandy
Tallmage, Pamela
Craghead, Tena Lucas
Miller, Linda May
Savory, Dorothy Keck
Hitchcock, Diana
Roth, Rose
Peterson, Maegan
Brown, Misti M.
Hansen, Sammy
Melius, Eva
Kohmetscher, Nancy
Gilmore, Mary
Hanna, Mary Mooreland
Wietzki, Carol
Tansey, Stacey
Monk, Shawn
Gledhill, Frances
Miller, Christy White
Fuller, Jennifer
Manero, Mary

To order more books go to: www.nprailfest.com

Powering UP: A History of the Women of the Union Pacific in North Platte, Nebraska